Armies of Ancient Greece

Armies of Ancient Greece

Circa 500 to 338 BC

Gabriele Esposito

Pen & Sword
MILITARY

First published in Great Britain in 2020 by
Pen & Sword Military
An imprint of
Pen & Sword Books Ltd
Yorkshire – Philadelphia

ISBN 978 1 52675 189 8

A CIP catalogue record for this book is
available from the British Library.

Typeset by Mac Style
Printed and bound in India by Replika Press Pvt. Ltd.

Pen & Sword Books Limited incorporates the imprints of Atlas, Archaeology,
Aviation, Discovery, Family History, Fiction, History, Maritime, Military, Military
Classics, Politics, Select, Transport, True Crime, Air World, Frontline Publishing,
Leo Cooper, Remember When, Seaforth Publishing, The Praetorian Press,
Wharncliffe Local History, Wharncliffe Transport, Wharncliffe True Crime
and White Owl.

For a complete list of Pen & Sword titles please contact

PEN & SWORD BOOKS LIMITED
47 Church Street, Barnsley, South Yorkshire, S70 2AS, England
E-mail: enquiries@pen-and-sword.co.uk
Website: www.pen-and-sword.co.uk

Or

PEN AND SWORD BOOKS
1950 Lawrence Rd, Havertown, PA 19083, USA
E-mail: Uspen-and-sword@casematepublishers.com
Website: www.penandswordbooks.com

Contents

Gabriele Esposito is a military historian who works as a freelance author and researcher for some of the most important publishing houses in the military history sector. In particular, he is an expert specializing in uniformology: his interests and expertise range from the ancient civilizations to modern post-colonial conflicts. During recent years he has conducted and published several researches on the military history of the Latin American countries, with special attention on the War of the Triple Alliance and the War of the Pacific. He is among the leading experts on the military history of the Italian Wars of Unification and the Spanish Carlist Wars. His books and essays are published on a regular basis by Osprey Publishing, Winged Hussar Publishing and Libreria Editrice Goriziana; he is also the author of numerous military history articles appearing in specialized magazines like *Ancient Warfare Magazine*, *Medieval Warfare Magazine*, *The Armourer*, *History of War*, *Guerres et Histoire*, *Focus Storia* and *Focus Storia Wars*.

Acknowledgements

This book is dedicated to my fantastic parents, Maria Rosaria and Benedetto, for the great love and fundamental support that they continue to give me every day. Thanks to their precious observations deriving from long experience, the present work is much more complete and easy to read.

A very special mention goes to the Spanish re-enactment group and living history association Athenea Prómakhos, for providing me with the magnificent and detailed photos that illustrate this book. Without their incredible work of research and re-enactment, the present work would have not been the same. In particular, I want to express my deep gratitude to Jonatan Prieto: he enjoyed and supported the idea of this book from the beginning and helped me in every phase of the production with great generosity and patience.

Introduction

During the long and crucial centuries of the Bronze Age (3,500–1,200 BC), Greece was home to two of the world's most ancient and important civilizations: the continental one of the Mycenaeans and the Minoan one centred on the island of Crete. The warlike Mycenaeans started to expand and conquered all the Minoan territories in a series of brutal military campaigns. The Mycenaeans were a great land power, while the Minoans had a created a wide naval empire that extended over most of the Aegean Sea. Mycenaean expansionism also affected other areas of the Mediterranean, such as the island of Cyprus and, most notably, the western part of Anatolia. The vast latter region was extremely rich in natural resources and was very important from a strategic point of view: it was a 'bridge' connecting the Aegean world with the great civilizations of the Ancient Middle East. At that time Anatolia was ruled by the Hittites, fierce warriors and brutal conquerors who had challenged the dominance of Egypt throughout the Middle East. The centre of the Hittites' power and their capital was in central Anatolia, but they also exerted direct control over the eastern region. In the western part of what later became Asia Minor was a league of twenty-two minor states known as the Assuwa Confederation. All the states that made up this military alliance were Hittite vassals, and thus the Assuwa Confederation can be considered as a 'buffer state' created by the Hittites in order not to have a long land border with the aggressive and expanding Mycenaeans. At the head of the Assuwa Confederation was probably the city of Troy, one of the richest and largest urban centres of western Anatolia. The Trojans, thanks to the strategic location of their city near the Hellespont and Dardanelles, controlled most of the commercial routes that crossed the region and had transformed their magnificent urban centre into the terminal of a formidable 'Bronze and Copper Road'. The latter started in the heart of Central Europe and followed the course of the Danube until reaching the Black Sea, where the precious metals from the northern Balkans were sold to the Trojan merchants who imported them into the 'civilized' world of Greece and the Middle East. The Mycenaeans wished to replace the Trojans as the 'masters of the metals' in the Aegean, and thus started to plan an invasion of the Assuwa Confederation. This would have probably caused a great clash with the Hittites, but the latter were heavily involved against Egypt and thus could not send large military forces against the Mycenaeans. The Mycenaeans first launched a

Greek hoplite with full
heavy infantry panoply.
(*Photo and copyright by
Athenea Prómakhos*)

series of raids against the main settlements on the Anatolian coast, before mounting an invasion. This ended with the conquest and destruction of Troy, presumably after a long struggle. These events, in particular the siege and burning of Troy, were later to become the core content of the *Iliad*. Much important information regarding the Mycenaean political situation at the time of the Trojan War is given to us by the so-called 'Catalogue of Ships' in the second book of the *Iliad*. This epic catalogue lists the contingents of the Greek army moving against Troy. It provides the places of origin of each contingent and the number of ships required to transport the men of each king to Troy. If taken to be an accurate account, it provides a rare summary of the geopolitical situation in Greece at some time before the end of the Late Bronze Age. It portrays a loose union of city-states, mostly located in mainland Greece, ruled by hereditary families under the overlordship of the 'High King' of Mycenae (the famous Agamemnon). In the *Iliad*, the Greek catalogue lists twenty-nine contingents under forty-six captains, accounting for a total of 1,186 ships. Using the figure of 100 men per ship, except for the Boeotian ones that had 120 men each, it results in a total of 120,000 warriors being transported to Anatolia. The Boeotians, including the Thebans, were said to have provided a total of 6,000 fighters and fifty ships; the Athenians sent 5,000 warriors with fifty ships; the Argives provided 8,000 warriors and eighty ships, the majority of these coming from Argos and Tiryns; Mycenae, the leading city of mainland Greece, sent the largest contingent with 10,000 fighters and 100 ships; the Spartans also provided a very large military force, with 6,000 warriors and sixty ships; Pylos, at that time an extremely important city, deployed 9,000 fighters and ninety ships; and the Mycenaean communities on Crete assembled a force of 8,000 warriors with eighty ships.

The last phase of Mycenaean expansion, which included the conquest of Troy, took place between the thirteenth and twelfth centuries BC, at the same time as Hittite expansionism reached its peak against Egypt. At this point, however, something very strange happened: the Mycenaeans went back to their homes in Greece without consolidating their conquests in western Anatolia; the Hittite Empire disappeared from history in just a few decades; and the Egyptians entered a terrible period of general decay. It was the end of the Bronze Age and the beginning of the new Iron Age. But which was behind all these incredible political changes? The answer to this question is not an easy one, but what we know for sure is that the many difficulties experienced by these three great civilizations were caused by an interminable series of invasions and raids launched by several 'new' peoples. The latters' warriors, equipped with new iron weapons, had a clear technical superiority over their opponents and thus were able to crush most of the armies that had traditionally dominated the Mediterranean. The companion piece to the *Illiad*, the *Odyssey*, contains indirect

Greek hoplite attacking with his spear. (*Photo and copyright by Athenea Prómakhos*)

information about these revolutionary events, since it reports that all the Mycenaean princes who returned to their homes after the Trojan War found their Greek kingdoms in complete turmoil. This could suggest that the first raids of these new peoples took place while the Mycenaean conquest of western Anatolia was still in the process of being completed. But who were these new peoples who demolished the Mycenaean and Hittite civilizations? According to most recent studies, they belonged to two main groups: the Dorians, who came from the heart of the Balkans and invaded Greece from the north, and the Sea Peoples, who came from Central Europe/the western Mediterranean and raided Greece from the south. Apparently both these groups were confederations of tribes, having different backgrounds but many elements in common, all searching for new lands to conquer. The Sea Peoples, who directed their attacks against Anatolia, Syria, Phoenicia, Canaan, Cyprus and Egypt, were a naval power that could count on very large military fleets and thus could easily move from one area of the eastern Mediterranean to another. The Hittite Empire crumbled under their attacks, as well as the consolidated Mycenaean influence over the large island of Cyprus. In Egypt, however, the Sea Peoples, after some initial successes, were defeated by the pharaohs. Despite this setback, some of these warrior tribes were able to settle and create new states in the Middle East, such as the Philistines who settled in Canaan.

Greek hoplite
with Chalcidian
helmet. (*Photo and
copyright by Athenea
Prómakhos*)

Greek hoplite with a Hydra emblem painted on the shield. (*Photo and copyright by Athenea Prómakhos*)

Detail of a linothorax reinforced by bronze scales. (*Photo and copyright by Athenea Prómakhos*)

Greek hoplite with a crab emblem painted on the shield. (*Photo and copyright by Athenea Prómakhos*)

During the early Iron Age, the Sea Peoples launched many major raids against the Greek coast, but never managed to create a stable settlement. Their constant presence and menace, however, was a key factor in the development of a new phase in Greek history.

The Dorians, meanwhile, were able to conquer most of Greece after several decades of violent incursions, and thus became the founding community of the later Greek civilization. It is not clear from which area of the Balkans the Dorians came, but what we do know is that before the start of their invasions they were settled in the mountains of Epirus in the west and Macedonia in the east. From these poor areas they moved south, in search of new and prosperous lands to conquer. Thanks to their superior weaponry, the Dorians occupied most of Greece around 1,100–1,000 BC: western and central Greece and the Peloponnese became the centres of their power. In the Peloponnese, the Dorians conquered or founded some of the most important cities of ancient Greece, such as Sparta, Argos and Corinth. Their arrival in Greece, however, also caused the birth of another two important groups: the Aeolians and the Ionians. These were both formed by Mycenaean communities who survived the Dorian invasion and continued to keep some distinctive features, but which soon became quite different from their ancestors due to the strong influence exerted by the newcomers. The Aeolians retained control of Thessaly and Boeotia, two very important regions of eastern Greece, while the Ionians were settled on the large island of Euboea and on the Cyclades. As a result of this situation, the Dorians, Aeolians and Ionians became the three founding groups of the new Greek civilization. Each of them spoke a different language, and these idioms later transformed themselves into the three main dialects of the Greek language (Doric, Aeolic and Ionic). From 900–800 BC, all these three ethnic groups started to expand outside mainland Greece, colonizing important new territories. The Dorians, who had already occupied Crete and Rhodes, founded new settlements in southern Italy; the Aeolians colonized the northern Anatolian coast (which thus became known as Aeolia); and the Ionians did the same with the southern Anatolian coast (which became known as Ionia). The Aeolians and Ionians continued the expansionism of their Mycenaean ancestors in Anatolia, but this time they were able to found permanent settlements. As a result of this colonization, the Aegean became a Greek 'lake' and the centre of a new civilization.

The period described above, lasting from 1,100–800/700 BC, is commonly known as the Greek Dark Ages or Greek Middle Ages, because it was a difficult phase of transition between the Mycenaean civilization and the new Classical Greek one. These three or four centuries were characterized by a series of deep changes that affected Greek society in many areas, including artistically and militarily. The Greek Dark Ages are also known as the Geometric Period, because of the artistic decorations that

Greek hoplite equipped with a nice example of linothorax. (*Photo and copyright by Athenea Prómakhos*)

Greek hoplite in attack position. (*Photo and copyright by Athenea Prómakhos*)

became popular during this time, or as the Homeric Age, since it was during those centuries that the famous Homeric poems were composed. This age still contained many elements deriving from the Mycenaean period, albeit mixed with some new ones brought by the Dorians. Mycenaean society had for centuries been dominated by the figure of the 'wanax', or king, a powerful aristocrat and warlord who could count on the support of a personal retinue formed by several professional warriors. In addition, each wanax controlled his realm from fortified palaces and citadels that were protected by gigantic 'cyclopic' walls. With the Doric invasion, such settlements entered a process of rapid decay: the walled citadels and monumental palaces built by

Greek *Ekdromos* with no armour. (*Photo and copyright by Athenea Prómakhos*)

the Mycenaeans were abandoned, replaced by new cities that gradually developed from the small villages created by the newcomers. There is no doubt that this era of Greek history had some 'dark' features, like the frequent naval raids of the Sea Peoples, but it would be a mistake to perceive it as a totally negative period of transformation. It was during the Greek Middle Ages, in fact, that most of the Classical Greek civilization's main features were shaped and firmly established.

The complex political and military organization of the Mycenaeans disappeared, together with any form of centralized authority. Mycenaean writing, the famous 'Linear-B' system, was also abandoned, replaced by a new Phoenician alphabet that gave birth to all the following alphabets in the world's history. These material and cultural changes were enormous, causing a revolution in all the fields of human knowledge. By the beginning of the eighth century BC, however, a new and very positive age began in the history of Greece: the economy and commerce started to flourish again thanks to the stabilization following the end of the foreign invasions, the population began to grow very rapidly, and this gave a great impulse to the process of colonization that had already started. For the first time in many centuries, Greece became over-populated and thousands of inhabitants thus had to move outside their traditional territories, founding new Greek cities, or colonies, across the Mediterranean. The main targets of Greek expansionism were the coasts of Anatolia and southern Italy; the former became known as Asia Minor while the colonies created in Italy became collectively known as Magna Grecia. The Greek settlers soon transformed their colonies into rich and prosperous commercial centres, all part of the new economic network that the Greek civilization was organizing in the Mediterranean. They even founded new cities in Libya, western Spain, southern France and southern Crimea. In doing so they found a new enemy in the Phoenicians, who were doing more or less the same: a new power struggle for dominance over the Mediterranean thus started. This would last for centuries and would have Sicily as its main battlefield; it was there that the most important colonies of Magna Grecia faced the most powerful of the Phoenician colonies, Carthage.

During most of the Greek Dark Ages, after the fall of the so-called 'palatial society' of the Mycenaeans, the communities inhabiting Greece were organized in a quite rudimentary way. Society was based on the *oikos*, a sort of familial clan or group that comprised all the inhabitants of the same village/small city. Each *oikos* was a little tribe and was guided by a king (*basileus*), an aristocrat who ruled thanks to his military capabilities. Over time, the villages started to expand and became proper cities: as a result, each of them comprised several *oikos* clans and was ruled by an assembly of aristocrats. Most of the new Greek cities were therefore not under the dominance of a single monarch, but of oligarchies, formed by the most wealthy and influential aristocrats. Since the economic resources of these new communities were quite scarce, during the Greek Dark Ages warfare was usually restricted to a very small and local scale. Each *oikos* was at war with its bordering clans, but generally military operations were conducted by very small numbers of men and had only minor objectives. The raiding of livestock and the pursuit of other booty were the main reasons behind the outbreak of these wars. The leaders of each *oikos* were warlords and thus always wished to augment their personal power by launching small raids and incursions. From a political point of view, there was a lot of fragmentation, so it is impossible to identify any dominant or ruling city in the Greece of these turbulent years. The Greek armies of this period were formed by a few hundred warriors: the *basileus* was followed by his personal retainers, who were all minor aristocrat warlords (*aristoi*) and were in turn followed by other personal retainers of lesser social status. When the figure of the *basileus* disappeared, the *aristoi* started to assemble their forces only for military campaigns and elected temporary supreme commanders (in charge only for the duration of the hostilities). The noble warriors were still equipped more or less as the Mycenaean ones from the late Bronze Age, but iron had rapidly replaced bronze as the main metal used in the production of weapons. There were no group tactics to speak of, since battles usually fragmented themselves into a series of duels between single aristocratic 'champions'. These went to the field of battle mounted on

Greek *Ekdromos*; note the detail of the back of the *hoplon* shield. (*Photo and copyright by Athenea Prómakhos*)

Greek *Ekdromos* with bronze greaves, which were rarely worn by the lightly equipped *ekdromoi.* (*Photo and copyright by Athenea Prómakhos*)

Greek *Ekdromos* attacking with his spear. (*Photo and copyright by Athenea Prómakhos*)

war chariots or on horses, accompanied by their servants, but always dismounted to fight. Warfare, in general, retained many similarities to that described in the famous Homeric poems. Missile weapons like bows and slings had only a secondary role, cavalry tactics were non-existent and chariots were not used as mobile platforms to fire arrows (as happened in the Middle East, for example). In this regard, it should be remembered that the geography of Greece (mostly mountains and hills) was not particularly suitable for the employment of large cavalry or chariot contingents (with the notable exception of the Thessalian plains). All this was to change dramatically with the birth of hoplite warfare, involving a new kind of citizen-warrior, which was a result of the creation of the new political system based on the city-state (*polis*) around the middle of the seventh century BC.

Chapter 1

The Birth of the *Polis* and the Hoplite

Between the eighth and seventh century BC, the small *oikos* communities started to disappear from several areas of Greece, replaced by larger cities that comprised the inhabitants of several villages. Thanks to a general improvement in the economy and commerce because of the political instability caused by foreign invasions, the Greeks started to feel the need for much larger and more stable institutions that could govern the new social changes (which were taking place very rapidly). Most of the new cities, or *poleis*, were founded during this crucial period, but some of them had also been inhabited during the 'dark ages'. Initially the early *polis* continued to be ruled by a *basileus*, but they were soon replaced by oligarchic forms of government controlled by the *aristoi*. Over time the power of the aristocracy also started to be reduced, gradually substituted by that of the tyrants, demagogic dictators who could count on the support of the low-ranking social classes. The tyrants' political phase, however, did not last for long, and by the beginning of the fifth century BC a number of Greek cities (including Athens) had adopted a democratic form of government. With the creation of the early *polis*, most of the villages disappeared and the *oikos* communities resettled inside the new urban centres. As a result, a new military system had to be created in order to guarantee the defence of the cities: the few ruling aristocrats could not raise substantial military forces and thus could not protect the expanding interests of their *poleis*. Commerce and colonization were becoming increasingly important activities, which involved hundreds of merchants and artisans: economic rivalries between nearby cities began to develop, as well as political struggles inside the same cities. Each *polis* was an autonomous state that controlled the surrounding portion of countryside; as a result, each city-state now needed autonomous military institutions. Basically, each able-bodied male living in a *polis* was a potential soldier and thus had to serve for the defence of his state as a citizen-soldier, a fighter whose right to be a citizen and whose social position were strongly linked to his military obligations. Those who were not able to serve in the military due to their age or to physical reasons were not considered as proper citizens. In addition, especially at the beginning of this new historical period, the personal economic position of each individual played a very important role in determining his military function. Only those few men who were rich enough to buy the full panoply of a heavy infantryman could be considered as full citizens. The poorer individuals could serve only with auxiliary roles and thus had little importance in the political assemblies. The position occupied in the army reflected the wealth of a man, while his political rights were directly linked to the economic capabilities of an individual. This would change only in later times, when the full development of democracy led the various cities to implement important military reforms. According to these, the government of each *polis* would give full military equipment to those citizens who could not afford to buy and maintain it. The fact that weapons could now be carried by every able-bodied male citizen, and not only by the aristocrats, led to a revolution: the individual fighting skills and military privileges of previous ages were abandoned, since each fighter was now equal to his companions. There were no more *aristoi* and retainers: all soldiers had the same importance and dignity, which derived from their economic capabilities. A member of an aristocratic family could now fight side-by-side with a merchant or an artisan who had become rich enough to buy the full military panoply. The new figure of a soldier that corresponded to the citizen-soldier was the hoplite: basically, a heavy infantryman with standard equipment. The central element of his panoply was the round shield, or *hoplon*, which gave the hoplites their name. The use of the *hoplon*, also known as the 'Argive shield' since it was probably designed for the first time in Argos, enabled citizen-soldiers to fight in a new close formation known as the phalanx, which generally had a rectangular shape. It consisted of several lines of heavy infantrymen, protecting each other with their round shields and forming a wall. This was defended by the primary weapon of each hoplite, the long spear, upon which most Greek tactics of the time were based. Each hoplite also carried a short sword, but this was a secondary weapon employed only for close combat or when the spear was broken. The defensive equipment of each soldier was completed by a helmet and a cuirass.

While these changes took place in the military field, some Greek cities started to emerge as regional powers after launching campaigns of conquest. For reasons of space, in the present book we will follow the military achievements of just five of the major Greek cities: Athens, Sparta, Thebes, Argos and Corinth. Some of these had common military features, while others were totally different. All of them, however, exerted a considerable military influence over most of the minor Greek *poleis*. Athens had already been a very important urban centre during the Mycenaean period, since it had a major fortress on the site of the famous Acropolis, defended by massive walls. In addition, on the Acropolis was a large palace that had been inhabited by a powerful *wanax*. Athens was not particularly affected by the Doric invasions, since the newcomers were not able to establish permanent settlements in Attica (the region of Athens). In addition, Athens was one of the first Greek cities to recover from the economic stagnation that characterized most of the early 'dark ages'. By the beginning

Greek *Ekdromos* with Attic helmet. (*Photo and copyright by Athenea Prómakhos*)

Greek hoplite with full heavy infantry panoply. (*Photo and copyright by Athenea Prómakhos*)

Greek hoplite with scorpion emblem painted on the shield. (*Photo and copyright by Athenea Prómakhos*)

of the ninth century, the Athenians were already among the best merchants and artisans of mainland Greece, and their influence was rapidly growing. Until the ninth century, the city of Athens was ruled by kings, who were at the head of a powerful land-owning aristocracy. This Athenian *aristoi* formed a council known as the *Areopagus* and had distinctive expansionist behaviours. Within a few decades they were able to conquer most of the minor settlements located in Attica and put them under the political control of their city. Around 622 BC the *Areopagus*, facing increasing social unrest among the citizens, decided to give a written constitution to Athens and to reform several aspects of society. This event marked the beginning of a new age in the history of the city. Like Athens, Sparta had also been a very important centre during the Mycenaean period: Menelaus, brother of the Mycenaean supreme leader Agamemnon and husband of the famous Helen of Troy, had been one of the Spartan kings. With the Doric invasion of the Peloponnese, Sparta was one of the first major Greek cities to be conquered by the newcomers. The previous Mycenaean settlement was destroyed and the Dorians assumed complete control of the territory. In a very short time, Sparta became the centre of Doric power in Greece. This was something that always differentiated the Spartans from other Greeks, especially from a cultural point of view. No other city in Greece had such a strong Doric heritage as Sparta. Traditionally, the 'new' Sparta was created from the fusion of two Doric villages, which would explain why the city was ruled by two kings and not by a single one. Later, another two villages were absorbed into the new *polis*, and as a result the inhabitants of Sparta started to be traditionally divided into four tribes (each of these deriving from one of the previous Doric villages). Around 820 BC, the Spartans started to feel the need for a written constitution that could regularize the political and social life of their growing community, similarly to what happened in Athens two centuries later. In both cities the first form of constitution was written by famous and semi-legendary lawgivers: Lycurgus in Sparta and Draco in Athens. With the legislative reforms of Lycurgus, the proper history of Classical Sparta began.

Thebes was one of the most important cities of Mycenaean Greece, much more so than Athens or Sparta. According to the most recent finds and excavations, the city was founded together with the earliest Mycenaean settlements of mainland Greece, or even before them. It seems that Thebes was the first 'super-power' of Greece and thus exerted a political dominance over the rest of the Mycenaean world. At a certain point, not long before the conquest and burning of Troy, the emerging city of Mycenae challenged the supremacy of Thebes and formed a large anti-Theban military alliance. During the ensuing war, the Thebans were defeated and the cyclopic walls of their city were destroyed. As a result, by the time the Trojan War broke out, the Greek world was guided by Mycenae, while Thebes had been reduced to the status of a secondary

Greek hoplite in attack position. (*Photo and copyright by Athenea Prómakhos*)

centre. The war conducted by Mycenae and other cities against Thebes probably gave origin to the famous myth of the 'Seven against Thebes', which describes the fall of the Theban hegemony. Thebes was probably occupied, albeit for a brief period, by the Dorians, but evidence to support this view is quite scarce. What we know for sure is that the Thebans were then ruled by a very powerful land-owning aristocracy, having strong expansionist ambitions.:The Thebans soon started to expand their sphere of influence over most of Boeotia. Differently from the Athenians, however, the absorption of the smaller communities into the larger city proved to be very difficult. The minor cities were obliged to join a Boeotian League guided by Thebes, but never renounced their formal autonomy and always remained distinct political entities. Around 506 BC, the Thebans started to look towards Attica for their expansion and thus a strong rivalry with Athens began.

Argos was already a very important city during the Mycenaean period, being one of the main allies of Mycenae in the struggle against Thebes. Before the ascendancy of Sparta at the end of the 'dark ages', Argos exerted a strong dominance over most of

Greek hoplite wearing
Corinthian helmet and
linothorax. (*Photo and
copyright by Athenea
Prómakhos*)

Greek hoplite
with leather
cuirass and
Attic helmet.
The helmet has
cheek pieces of
the same kind
usually hinged
to Phrygian/
Thracian
helmets. (*Photo
and copyright
by Athenea
Prómakhos*)

the northern Peloponnese and was one of the greatest military powers of Greece. Like Sparta, Argos was occupied by the Dorians and thus had a very distinct Doric nature for most of the following centuries. The city gradually acquired control over the vast and fertile plain of Argolid, one of the most prosperous regions of Greece. By around 660 BC, the Argives had become powerful and rich enough to challenge Sparta for dominance over the Peloponnese, launching a series of expansionist campaigns under the leadership of their monarch Pheidon (Argos was ruled by kings for a long time, being one of the last Greek cities to abandon this form of government). Corinth, unlike the other four cities described above, did not exist during the Mycenaean period. The strategic area of Greece located around the Isthmus of Corinth was sparsely inhabited before the arrival of the Dorians, who understood that a new settlement located near the isthmus could become extremely rich thanks to its position. The isthmus was the only land bridge connecting the Peloponnese to the rest of mainland Greece. As a result, around 900 BC, the Dorians created the first basic settlement of what would later become the city of Corinth. In the eighth century BC, the initial small urban

Greek hoplite attacking with his spear. (*Photo and copyright by Athenea Prómakhos*)

Greek hoplite in full heavy infantry panoply. (*Photo and copyright by Athenea Prómakhos*)

Greek hoplite with Corinthian helmet and linothorax. (*Photo and copyright by Athenea Prómakhos*)

centre developed very rapidly under the guidance of the Bacchiadae Doric clan, who expanded the dominance of Corinth over nearby villages and created a 'royal house'. During these years, due to a massive growth of population, the Corinthians also played a prominent role in the Greek colonization of the Mediterranean (much more than other cities like Argos, for example). In 747 BC, however, the Corinthian *aristoi* revolted against the Bacchiadae kings and transformed their city into an oligarchy. This form of government was soon also abandoned, with the ascendancy of the first Corinthian tyrant. As we will see, during the seventh and sixth century BC, all five cities described above would enter into a new and massive expansionist phase that would shape the political map of Greece for decades. The new wars of this age were not fought only by hoplites, since they took place at the same time as the general transition from the old military system of the 'dark ages' to the new one of Classical Greece.

Chapter 2

The Ascendancy of Sparta

By the fifth century BC, the city of Sparta had become the greatest military power of Greece and the ruling centre of the Peloponnese region, but these great achievements were reached only after almost three centuries of incessant warfare that forged the Spartan 'national' spirit. The Spartans called their city Lakedaimon and referred to themselves using the term Lakedaimonians: both these words derived from Lakonia, the name of the region where the city of Sparta was located in the southern Peloponnese. At the time of the city's re-founding, however, the Spartans did not even control the whole territory of Lakonia and were just a minor centre in an area that was dominated by other powers. Bearing this in mind, how was it possible for the future Lakedaimonians to become a great military power and emerge as the only true warrior community of Greece? To find an answer to this question, it is necessary to go back to the early days of the 'new' city, and in particular to the period during which Lycurgus gave to Sparta a first form of written constitution. The first of Lycurgus' reforms involved the formation of a new council of elders known as the Gerousia: this comprised twenty-eight *aristoi*, who came from the most important families of the Spartan nobility. Each of them had equal powers and their main function was to mediate between the two kings (Sparta was ruled by the peculiar dual monarchy for many decades) and the community of the ordinary citizens. From a formal point of view, the members of the royal houses were not superior to the members of the Gerousia, who controlled the political life of the city, promulgated the new laws and took the most important decisions. Some of these decisions, such as declaring war on a foreign enemy, had to be voted on by the whole body of the citizens before being approved. However, it was the Gerousia that could propose arguments to be voted and thus the body of the citizens could not express itself in an autonomous way. The second measure introduced by Lycurgus affected the division of lands and properties among the citizens. In order to avoid the outbreak of social clashes, caused by the enormous disparities existing between the aristocrats and the other citizens, it was decided to divide all the lands and properties in an equal way so that each member of the citizenship was perfectly equal to all the others. This measure, adopted only in Sparta, was an early example of 'distributism' and transformed the Spartans into a community of *Homoioi* (i.e. peers, or men of equal status). As a result, the citizens

Greek hoplite with bull emblem painted on the shield. (*Photo and copyright by Athenea Prómakhos*)

Nice example of archaic Corinthian helmet, with a single tall crest. (*Photo and copyright by Athenea Prómakhos*)

Greek light infantry javelineer. (*Photo and copyright by Athenea Prómakhos*)

started to consider themselves as an elite and formed a very compact social group. All of them became minor aristocrats, and thus there was no difference between rich *aristoi* and common citizens. After this reform, the *Homoioi* started to be commonly known as Spartiates and gradually transformed themselves into the best warriors in Greece. In exchange for receiving land and properties, each Spartan male had to dedicate his entire life to the military defence of the state.

Lycurgus also established the rigorous system of military education that made Sparta famous around the world: the *Agoge*. According to this, when a boy was born he had to be examined by the members of the Gerousia in order to determine if he would be able to serve in the army for the rest of his life. If the baby did not look fit for his future duties, he would be left alone at the base of Mount Taygetus for several days in a terrible test. Only if the baby survived (something that only happened quite rarely) would he then be educated as a Spartiate. On most occasions the babies left on the mountain died from exposure or were killed by wild animals, but as most of them had some kind of physical problems they were thus of no use according to the terrible and cruel laws of the Spartiates. At the age of 7, each boy was obliged to abandon his family and had to live together with all the other male children of his age under the supervision of a specific magistrate, charged with the education of the future warriors. The boys had to spend all the hours of the day together, doing exactly the same things: any form of individualism was rejected and all the young males were obliged to live in a very austere way, receiving only one red cloak from the state each year and not being allowed to wear anything different. The boys had to create their own beds out of reeds pulled by hand from the Eurotas River, and were intentionally underfed in order to encourage them to learn how to survive with practically no food. At the age of 12, the young Spartiates initiated their intensive military training, conducted on a daily basis, and each of them was assigned to an older tutor, a sort of instructor or protector. This system was created to secure the passage of military knowledge from one generation to another and to create strong personal links between all the members of the Spartan Army.

At the age of 18, each young Spartiate entered into the military 'reserve' and thus could be employed in case of war or emergency. Two years later, when aged 20, he would officially become a member of the Spartan Army after receiving his shield from the state during a public ceremony. After having spent most of his life living in public barracks with other boys, at this point each Spartiate could initiate his own individual life by being admitted into one of the public assemblies. These were known as messes in Sparta, formed by male citizens who always ate together and who contributed equally in providing the food for their own assembly. The members of these political associations usually developed strong relationships between themselves, and also served side-by-side on the field of battle. Each new member of a mess had to be accepted by the other components of the group with a unanimous vote; if a Spartiate reached the age of 30 without having been admitted to any mess, he would not have gained full citizenship. At the age of 30, each Spartiate could finally marry and create a family of his own, and in addition he could now hold public offices since he had gained full citizenship. Once married, each young Spartiate had formally completed his *Agoge* and could be considered as part of an elite. Most of the years of the *Agoge* were spent by the young recruits undergoing daily intensive physical training. They marched for hours, learned how to use weapons, were instructed in combat tactics, fought in simulated battles and were encouraged to compete in any kind of athletic activities. Very little space was saved for the 'formation of the spirit', since a good Spartiate was judged only for his physical skills. Most of the citizens, in fact, were illiterate, unlike what happened in other Greek cities, where rhetoric and philosophy were considered as fundamental components of a boy's education. The impressive bodies of the Spartiates were forged by countless hours of training, which included the practising of several sports as well as undergoing frequent (and terrible) tests. Bearing all this in mind, it is not difficult to understand why Sparta became the greatest military power in Greece. The Spartiates formed a permanent military force made up of professional fighters, and no other city in Greece could field such a corps. They were not particularly numerous, since the *Agoge* was particularly selective, but they did compensate their few numbers with superior skills. The education system introduced by Lycurgus transformed Sparta into a military community, but did have some negative effects on the economy of the city: during their life, the Spartiates were not permitted to work as peasants or as artisans; in addition, they could not trade as merchants with foreign states. This meant that the Spartan economy was extremely poor, something that affected the daily life of most of the citizens. The Spartan constitution introduced by Lycurgus remained unchanged for centuries, the only modification to the system described above being the later creation of the Ephors. These were five supreme magistrates, elected every year and forming an executive council. They reached such a position thanks to their personal merits and not because of their family origins. The Ephors were introduced some 130 years after the reforms of Lycurgus in an attempt to further reduce the power of the kings. In practice, the Ephors assumed all the executive powers previously hold by the monarchs and thus established a form of oligarchic government, with the kings retaining only ceremonial functions.

Thanks to their superior military system, the Spartiates soon started to launch major campaigns of conquest in the territories surrounding their city. They needed new lands for the production of food as well as a sufficient number of subjugated enemies who could work as peasants on these lands. The first Spartan campaigns resulted in

Greek light skirmisher throwing one of his javelins. (*Photo and copyright by Athenea Prómakhos*)

the conquest of Lakonia, which was achieved with no particular difficulties. At this point, the Spartans turned their attention to the rich and fertile region of Messenia, located west of Lakonia in the southern Peloponnese. The First Messenian War began in 743 BC and lasted until 724 BC, resulting in a decisive Spartan victory. As a first move, the Spartiates occupied the important Messenian city of Ampheia and transformed it into their main military base in the region. At that time Messenia was ruled by a single monarch and was organized in a quite archaic way as a small kingdom. The Messenians, surprised by the initial Spartan attack, decided to gather all their available manpower to face the foreign invasion. All able-bodied citizens were given weapons and underwent some form of military training. The Messenian king, however, initially preferred to rely on his fortifications instead of facing the Spartans on the open field.

Greek peltast with javelins and *pelte* shield. (*Photo and copyright by Athenea Prómakhos*)

Greek peltast throwing one of his javelins. (*Photo and copyright by Athenea Prómakhos*)

In the summer of 739 BC, the Messenians moved against Ampheia with the objective of destroying the enemy stronghold, from which the Spartans had launched many incursions and raids.

Despite Spartan opposition, the Messenians were able to build a fortified camp near Ampheia and prepared themselves for a pitched battle. This was won by the Spartiates thanks to their superior military tactics: apparently this was the first battle in Greek history during which the phalanx formation was employed by one of the sides. Before this clash, the Spartans had already adopted the hoplite close formation and thus deployed their infantry in a single phalanx. The Messenians, instead, still fought according to the traditional tactics of the 'dark ages' and attacked the enemy without any kind of order. We don't know exactly when the Spartans introduced the phalanx formation into their military system, but their new hoplite formations surely proved fundamental in defeating the Messenians. According to the description by Pausanias of the battle between Spartiates and Messenians, it seems that the new hoplite tactics of the Spartans were still at a very basic stage of development. As a result, we could conclude that they had been introduced only shortly before 740 BC. The successes of the Spartiates' heavy infantrymen made a great echo around Greece and led to the gradual diffusion of the hoplite military system in most of the existing

Detail of a composite cuirass, basically a linothorax reinforced with bronze scales on the waist. (*Photo and copyright by Athenea Prómakhos*)

Nice example of a
Corinthian helmet.
(*Photo and copyright by
Athenea Prómakhos*)

Greek hoplite equipped with full panoply; his shield is painted with the emblem of the Medusa. (*Photo and copyright by Athenea Prómakhos*)

cities. Some scholars have argued that the birth of these tactics was the direct result of the equalitarian social reforms introduced by Lycurgus, but there is insufficient proof to support this view. What we know for sure is that Pausanias' account of the First Messenian War is the first written text describing the deployment of a phalanx. Within more or less a century, the hoplite became the standard fighter of each Greek army, starting to be depicted on several vases around 650 BC.

The conquest of Lakonia and Messenia had extremely important consequences for the society of Sparta, since it enabled the Spartiates to count on large amounts of defeated enemies who were transformed into subjects and could be employed as peasant workers to sustain the Spartan war economy. After the end of these early campaigns of conquest, the Spartiates created two new classes inside their society in order to assimilate the defeated communities of Lakonia and Messenia: the Helots and the *Perioikoi*. Among these two groups, the Helots had an inferior social status, being halfway between the condition of slaves and that of free men. They were tied to the land that they inhabited before the Spartan conquest and were a property of the Spartan state, just like the land; they could not abandon their villages and were forced to work as peasants for their entire life. Thanks to their agricultural production, the elite Spartiates could survive and even flourish without working. The Helots had no political rights and could not bear arms. A Spartiate could kill one of them even without a proper reason, and they had no possibility to improve their social position. The Helots were much more numerous than the Spartiates, but lived in conditions of complete misery. As a result, keeping the Helot population in check and preventing Helot rebellions became the two main concerns of the Spartan government. A series of measures were introduced to prevent rebellions from the subjugated populations, including the creation of a special secret police known as the *Crypteia* as well as the introduction of ritual demonstrations. Every autumn, for example, the Spartans ritually declared war on the Helots, and for an entire night they ravaged the latter's villages just to show again who were the masters. Killing a Helot was seen as something extremely positive for the early career of a Spartiate, since the Helots were considered to be always on the verge of rebellion. Each member of the *Crypteia* was authorized to execute any Helot suspected of treason, without requiring any proof: this secret police was specifically organized to prevent peasant uprisings in Lakonia and Messenia. Fear was the key factor dominating the relationships that existed between Spartans and Helots. The Helots were always waiting for the right moment, such as a foreign attack, to rise in open revolt against their masters. Despite not being slaves, the Helots were treated in an extremely harsh and cruel way by the Spartans, who used corporal punishment every day to maintain discipline. Each Spartiate had a certain number of Helots at his disposal. They were distributed among the Spartiates in an equal way, exactly like the conquered lands. The territories of Lakonia and Messenia were divided into several farms, all of the same size, known as *kleroi*. Each of the *kleroi* included a certain number of Helots. A predetermined portion of the harvest produced in each *kleros* was given to the Spartiate owner, with the little surplus that remained being used by the Helots to survive with their families. In time of war, each Helot was to act as a servant for his master and carry the latter's weapons and baggage.

The other new social group that emerged after the end of the First Messenian War was that of the *Perioikoi*. Unlike the Helots, these were free 'non-citizen' inhabitants of the Spartan state. They came from Lakonian or Messenian communities that had been absorbed into the dominions of Sparta but which had not been formally subjugated after a military defeat. Several communities of Lakonia and Messenia accepted Spartan suzerainty without fighting in order to preserve the 'free' personal status of their members. Differently from the Helots, who were mostly peasants, the *Perioikoi* had a very precise role in the Spartan society: they were to act as artisans and merchants, something that was forbidden to the Spartiates. As a result, they occupied a much better social position than the Helots and enjoyed a series of privileges, for example being allowed to travel outside Spartan territory to operate as merchants. The *Perioikoi* were not citizens, but played an extremely important role in Sparta's economy. They lived in separate settlements that enjoyed some form of local autonomy on domestic issues. Unlike the Helots, they contributed to the Spartan military system by sending contingents of hoplites and could own some land. One of the *Perioikoi*'s most important functions, especially from a military point of view, was that of producing weapons for the Spartiates. Like the Helots, however, these artisans and merchants were not permitted to vote or to hold public offices. Initially, the *Perioikoi* hoplites did fight in separate units, but as time progressed they were mixed with the Spartiates, whose numbers declined very rapidly due to successive wars.

After the end of the First Messenian War, Sparta started to expand towards the northern part of the Peloponnese. This region had traditionally been dominated by Argos, which was one of the major Greek military powers of the time. During the first half of the seventh century BC, the city of Argos was ruled by Pheidon, a monarch with great personal abilities and significant military skills. During the early phase of his long reign, Pheidon did his best to stop the ascendancy of Corinth and thus increase Argive dominance over the northern Peloponnese. He ruled the Argolid as a tyrant, enjoying great popular support, despite being a member of a very important noble family from Argos. In 669 BC, Pheidon had to face a massive Spartan invasion from the south. The Spartiates hoped to defeat Argos as they had already done with Messenia, and thus establish their own suzerainty over the rich territory of Argolis. By that time, however, the Argive army had also adopted hoplite tactics and formations, so the Spartans did

Greek hoplite with no
armour; this was the kind
of personal equipment
in use by the time of
the Peloponnesian War.
(*Photo and copyright by
Athenea Prómakhos*)

Greek hoplite with the emblem of the Pegasus winged horse painted on his shield. (*Photo and copyright by Athenea Prómakhos*)

Greek hoplite in attack position. (*Photo and copyright by Athenea Prómakhos*)

not have a clear military superiority. At the Battle of Hysiae, fought a few miles to the south-west of Argos, the invading Spartan army was soundly defeated by Pheidon. According to tradition, it was Pheidon who perfected the early hoplite formations by introducing the use of the round *hoplon* shield, and this was a key factor for the victory of the Argives in 669 BC. Until that time, the Spartans continued to employ shields with traditional shapes, albeit fighting in some sort of 'proto-phalanx' formation (as described in Pausanias' chronicle of the First Messenian War). In any case, the Argive victory stopped Spartan expansionism towards the Argolid and caused some serious troubles to the Spartiates: in 668 BC, most of the Helots rose in open revolt against Sparta, with the decisive support of Pheidon and the Argive Army. During this Second Messenian War, the Spartiates came very near to complete defeat on several occasions and the whole Spartan social system was on the verge of collapse. The Messenians reconquered their home territories, elected a new king and even invaded Lakonia. During the following years the Spartans were defeated by the Messenians in two pitched battles, while the Argives launched a series of strong incursions that ravaged most of the Spartan countryside. At some point, probably after Pheidon's death, the general situation of the conflict changed and the Messenians were obliged to adopt a new defensive attitude. The Spartiates were finally able to defeat the Messenians and quell the rebellion, bringing back all the defeated communities to their previous Helot status. After their victory in the Second Messenian War, the Spartiates did not face any further Helot revolts for many decades.

The rivalry with Argos for dominance over the Peloponnese, however, continued for a long time and caused the outbreak of several further wars between the two Doric cities. In 546 BC Sparta and Argos went to war over possession of the Thyrea Plain, but decided to avoid full-scale conflict: in order to decide which of the rivals would control the contested territory, it was agreed to organize an armed confrontation between 300 champions chosen from the Spartan army and 300 from the Argive army. This historical episode is reported by Herodotus, who describes it in detail. According to legend, after an entire day of brutal fighting, only three warriors survived: two Argives and one Spartan. As a result, this 'clash of champions' ended in a stalemate and both sides were forced to fight a proper pitched battle. This resulted in a clear Spartan victory and led to the Spartan annexation of the Thyrea Plain. In 494 BC, shortly before the outbreak of the First Persian War, the Spartans and Argives again went to war with each other. This time the conflict was not declared for possession of a specific territory, but was intended from the beginning as a decisive war to determine the destiny of the Peloponnese. During the previous decades, the Spartiates had greatly augmented their power and were now able to face the Argives with a marked superiority. Argos had started to suffer from the expansionism of Corinth and was gradually losing its prominent position. At the Battle of Sapeia in 494 BC, the Argive army was completely annihilated by the Spartiates. The clash was particularly violent, thousands of Argives were killed and, after such a defeat, Argos was unable to recover for many years. The city had lost a considerable amount of manpower, to the point that the Argives decided to remain neutral during the Persian Wars of 490–479 BC. Argos was only able to challenge the dominance of Sparta again after the outbreak of the Peloponnesian War (431–404 BC).

Traditionally, the Peloponnese was divided into six main regions: Lakonia and Messenia in the south (under the firm control of Sparta), Arcadia in the centre, Elis in the west, Achaea in the north and Argolis in the east (including Argos but also, at least initially, Corinth). As we have seen, the Spartans fought several wars against the city of Argos in order to establish their dominance over Argolis, but it should be remembered that the Spartiates also launched several military campaigns against Tegea (the most powerful and important of the Arcadian cities). In 550 BC a large pitched battle was fought between an alliance of Arcadian cities guided by Tegea and Sparta, which resulted in a clear Arcadian victory that stopped Spartan expansionism towards the central Peloponnese for some time. Since it was by now clear that Arcadia could never be annexed by the Spartans as they had done with Messenia, the Spartiates decided

Greek hoplite wearing a nice example of a Chalcidian helmet. (*Photo and copyright by Athenea Prómakhos*)

Greek hoplite equipped with Chalcidian helmet. (*Photo and copyright by Athenea Prómakhos*)

Greek hoplite with light
panoply. (*Photo and
copyright by Athenea
Prómakhos*)

to conclude a treaty with Tegea and form a military alliance with the Arcadian cities. Meanwhile, the Spartans tried to extend their political influence over the cities of Elis, in the western Peloponnese, and Corinth. The latter, after a brief period of oligarchic government, had started to be governed by tyrants such as the famous Cypselus, who ruled from 658–628 BC. During this period Corinth became one of the most over-populated *poleis* of Greece, and thus was one of the cities from which the highest number of emigrants departed. The Corinthian settlers created several new colonies abroad, founding the most important city of Magna Grecia, Syracuse, which would later become the ruling power of Greek Sicily. Cypselus tried to create a hereditary royal house in Corinth, but his heirs did not have his personal capabilities and were hated by most of the citizens. The Spartans, hoping to obtain some advantage from this situation, helped the Corinthian population to remove the Cypselid tyrants, and soon after these events, in 550 BC, Corinth became one of Sparta's main allies in the Peloponnese. Some years later, in 525 BC, Sparta and Corinth signed a new 'anti-Argive' military alliance. Thanks to the strategic location of their city, most of the Corinthians became extremely rich: they were excellent merchants and seamen, inventing the famous trireme warship and fighting the first naval battle recorded in Greek history. All the goods imported into or exported from the Peloponnese had to pass across the Isthmus of Corinth, and this enabled the Corinthians to become increasingly free from the original Argive political influence. During this same period, the Spartiates were able to expand their influence over Elis: their political support, in fact, proved to be decisive in securing control of the prestigious Olympic Games for Elis (the city of Olympia was located in the region of Elis). Around 550 BC, all the Peloponnesian allies of Sparta joined a new military alliance created by the Spartiates, known as the Peloponnesian League, with only Argos and the cities of Achaea not joining the coalition. Spartan dominance over the Peloponnese had finally been achieved.

Chapter 3

The Lelantine War and the Rise of Athens

As suggested in the previous chapter, the new military system based on hoplite warfare started to become widespread around 675–670 BC, with Sparta and Argos among the first important cities that reformed their own military forces. The transition from the post-Mycenaean individual fighter of the 'dark ages' to the citizen-hoplite, however, was quite a long and complicated process. In some areas of Greece, especially the most isolated ones, traditional tactics continued to be used for decades; also, the new equipment associated with hoplite warfare was not always immediately introduced, since we have examples of new phalanx formations being made up of heavy infantrymen still equipped with old models of shield (this being the case with the Spartan 'proto-phalanx' fighting in the First Messenian War). One of the first conflicts in the history of Ancient Greece during which both sides used 'proper' hoplite armies was the Lelantine War, which raged from 710–650 BC. By the end of the conflict, both sides were deploying sizeable contingents of hoplites that used phalanx tactics. The Lelantine War involved the clash between the *poleis* of Chalcis and Eretria, both located on the strategically important island of Euboea, one of the largest islands in the Aegean Sea, located near mainland Greece and practically bordering both Boeotia and Attica. The conflict was fought for possession of the fertile Lelantine Plain, which was located in the middle of Euboea, exactly halfway between the cities of Chalcis and Eretria. These cities, together with the other urban centres of Euboea, had become increasingly rich during the years that preceded the outbreak of the war. Thanks to their strategic position, both Chalcis and Eretria had started to exert a considerable economic influence over the commercial routes of the eastern Aegean. In particular, these two cities were strongly linked to the Greek colonies located on the coast of Asia Minor, in Aeolia and Ionia. In addition, both Chalcis and Eretria were active in the colonization of new territories outside Greece. As time progressed, conflict between them became inevitable, since both the *poleis* now wanted to have complete dominance over Euboea. Due to the political and economic importance of the two warring cities, the Lelantine War was one of the first conflicts in Greek history that saw the formation of large military alliances: both Chalcis and Eretria could count on the support of other allied *poleis*. According to ancient sources, the Lelantine War was the first conflict fought between two alliances and not single cities since the times of the Trojan War.

Greek hoplite attacking with his spear. (*Photo and copyright by Athenea Prómakhos*)

These sources also state that the conflict involved a clash between two armies mostly made up of heavy infantrymen, armed with spear and sword. Both Chalcis and Eretria were Ionic cities, like Athens, and thus shared a common culture; despite this, they fought to the death for several decades.

In Ancient Greece, where fertile land was extremely scarce, wars were frequently fought for possession of plains (as we have seen, this also happened between Sparta and Argos). We know very little about the development of the Lelantine War, but from a few fragmentary sources we can try to attempt a general reconstruction. At the beginning of the conflict both sides still had 'archaic' armies, but by the end of the war, in 650 BC, they mostly deployed hoplite contingents. The Lelantine War was not fought on a very large scale, since the manpower of the confronting sides was

Greek hoplite with full heavy infantry equipment. (*Photo and copyright by Athenea Prómakhos*)

Greek hoplite attacking with his *xiphos* short sword. (*Photo and copyright by Athenea Prómakhos*)

relatively limited. We know that Chalcis could field a maximum of 3,000 hoplites, 600 cavalrymen and sixty war chariots, while Eretria had a similar army, but with more cavalry and fewer hoplites. After a first inconclusive phase, during which neither side was able to gain the upper hand, both Chalcis and Eretria started to call for the support of their allies. At that time Eretria controlled some of the Cyclades and thus could easily receive reinforcements from Asia Minor, where the Eretrians were allied with the important city of Miletus. The Chalcidians were allies of Samos (located on the homonym island) and Thessaly (from where the best cavalrymen of Greece came). Some scholars, underlining the fact that the Lelantine War took place at the same time as the Second Messenian War, have suggested that the two conflicts were probably connected to each other. There are some proofs, in fact, that Sparta supported Chalcis and Argos backed Eretria. It is plausible, however, that this support was only a political and not a military one. The main enemy of Samos, the island-city of Aegina, probably sided with Eretria, while Corinth and Megara probably supported Chalcis, since Corinth was a strong competitor of Eretria. The Lelantine War ended with Chalcidian victory, but in reality both sides had lost most of the importance they had before the outbreak of the conflict.

For several decades the Ionian cities of Euboea had been the dominant powers in the eastern Aegean, especially from a naval and commercial point of view. The terrible losses suffered during the Lelantine War, however, relegated both Chalcis and Eretria to become only minor actors in the Greek political scene. Athens, Corinth and Miletus benefited greatly from this unexpected outcome of the long conflict, since they were able to fill the gap left by Chalcis and Eretria. While the events described above took place in Euboea, Athens developed greatly in many aspects, especially a socio-political one. Around 622/621 BC, the city received its first written constitution, known as the Draconian Constitution, from the celebrated legislator Draco. This introduced a series of fundamental innovations: the old oral laws, known and arbitrarily applied only by the few Athenian *aristoi*, were substituted by written laws that could be consulted by all the literate citizens. For the first time, murder and involuntary homicide were clearly distinguished, in order to reduce the violent abuses of the aristocrats. The Draconian Constitution, however, did not have only positive features. In general it was particularly harsh, for example prescribing the forcing into slavery of debtors who were not able to pay their creditors and the death penalty even for minor offences like stealing. Draco also created a new political assembly, distinct from the *Areopagus*, known as the Council of Four Hundred because it comprised 400 members elected by all the free citizens who could furnish themselves with a complete set of military equipment. As a result, each free citizen who was rich enough to buy the panoply of a hoplite could vote: a very early form of democracy was born, as a response to the

Greek hoplite with the emblem of a trireme warship painted on his shield. (*Photo and copyright by Athenea Prómakhos*)

Greek hoplite equipped with Corinthian helmet having a massive double crest. (*Photo and copyright by Athenea Prómakhos*)

Detail of a composite linothorax reinforced with bronze scales. (*Photo and copyright by Athenea Prómakhos*)

traditional power of the *Areopagus*. The Draconian Constitution, however, could not last for long without being updated, since Athenian society was changing very rapidly. The creation of the Council of Four Hundred was not enough to counterbalance the power of the *Areopagus* in the long run, and the punishments prescribed by Draco were seen as too harsh for the new times.

As a result, in 593/594 BC, the new lawmaker Solon was asked to create a new written constitution for Athens. According to the Solonian Constitution, all Athenian citizens were divided into four political classes according to the assessment of their personal properties, the standard unit for this assessment being the *medimnos*, which corresponded to 12 gallons of cereals. Those citizens who were valued at 500 *medimnoi* or more for each year were known as *pentakosiomedimnoi* and were eligible to serve as *strategoi* (generals); those valued at 300 *medimnoi* or more for each year were known as *hippeis* and had to serve as cavalrymen in the army; those valued at 200 *medimnoi* or more for each year were known as *zeugitai* and had to serve as hoplites in the army; and those valued at up to 199 *medimnoi* or less for each year were known as *thetes* and had no precise military obligations. The *thetes*, however, could volunteer as lightly armed auxiliaries in the army or as simple rowers in the navy. Members of the *pentakosiomedimnoi* were the only citizens who could be elected to the high office of archon. The archons, superior magistrates of the Athenian state, appeared around 682 BC; they were nine in total and shared a series of important judicial/military/ religious functions. Before Solon's reforms, the archons were elected annually by the *Areopagus* on the basis of their nobility or wealth, but with the new constitution, they were chosen from among the *pentakosiomedimnoi* by all the members of the three top classes (the *thetes* could not vote and were excluded from all public offices). The citizens of all four classes made up the *Ekklesia*, or general assembly. Each year 6,000 members of the *Ekklesia*, chosen by lot, formed a supreme court of justice known as the Heliaia that was charged with the specific function of judging the archons. Before Solon's reforms, the archons could be judged only by the *Areopagus* (and thus by their peers).

Bearing in mind all the above, it is easy to conclude that the Solonian Constitution was the first truly democratic one of Greece, yet its introduction caused two decades or so of social unrest in the short term. Neither the *aristoi* nor the *thetes* were satisfied and wanted something more: the aristocrats could not accept the fact that the middle class of the *zeugitai* could also hold important public offices, while the lesser social group, instead, wanted more power of representation. As a result, after the reforms of Solon, two main political parties emerged in Athens: the aristocrat party and the popular party. In 541 BC, after 20 years of social struggles, the popular party gained the upper hand and one of its most important members rose to power: Peisistratus, perhaps the

Greek hoplite employing his *xiphos* short sword, which was only rarely used as a slashing sword. (*Photo and copyright by Athenea Prómakhos*)

Greek hoplite equipped with leather cuirass. (*Photo and copyright by Athenea Prómakhos*)

Greek hoplite attacking with his *xiphos* sword. (*Photo and copyright by Athenea Prómakhos*)

most famous tyrant in the history of Ancient Greece. In the Greek context of the time, the word 'tyrant' did not have the same negative meaning as today: it indicated a politician who had been able to assume control of a city thanks to his demagogic abilities and the support of the common people. Peisistratus was the perfect example of a tyrant, taking power with force but being beloved by the citizens.

He did not abolish the Solonian Constitution from a formal point of view, but in practice he ruled as a dictator and made sure that his family held all the most important offices of the Athenian state. The years of Peisistratus' rule were a real 'golden age' for the city, which became a centre of culture, where the most important philosophers and thinkers of the time were active. In addition, Athens became the most important artistic centre of Greece, where the most innovative works of art were produced. Athenian vases, thanks to their superior quality and elaborate decorations, became extremely popular, being produced on a massive scale and exported to all corners of the Mediterranean. Athenian merchants started to be very active on all the commercial routes of the Aegean, exporting and importing every kind of product. The economy of the city flourished, enabling the state to build several new public buildings, including the first aqueduct. All Greece, with the exception of Sparta, looked to Athens as a model city-state to follow. Athenian ships were present in all the ports of the Mediterranean, bringing the economic and political influence of their home into the most important Greek colonies located overseas. In practice, the Athenians were building up a naval empire made up of economic and commercial networks.

Peisistratus died in 527 BC, being succeeded by his sons Hippias and Hipparchus, but they soon proved to be inadequate rulers since they lacked the intelligence of their father. In 514 BC, after some years of widespread malcontent, Hipparchus was assassinated. At this point Hippias, instead of leaving power, transformed himself into a proper dictator (in the modern sense of the term). Hippias was a bitter and cruel ruler, who imposed very heavy taxation on his citizens and frequently ordered the execution of all individuals who opposed his despotic rule. By 510 BC the situation had became unsustainable: most of the population was against Hippias, but the dictator still retained power, mostly thanks to the support of some aristocrats and of the Persian Empire. As we will see, Asia Minor had been recently conquered by the Persians, who were now turning their attention towards Greece. Hippias ordered the exile of those aristocratic families that opposed his rule and his new amicable relations with the Persians. Among these families was the important one of the Alcmaeonidaes, who had gone in exile to Sparta during the days of Peisistratus. They were able to gain the support of the Spartan king Cleomenes I, who was particularly worried about the possible formation of a new military alliance between Athens and Persia against the Spartiates. In 510 BC, a Spartan army invaded Attica and occupied Athens, defeating the military forces of Hippias. The dictator tried to resist on the Acropolis, but was finally forced to abandon the city and flee into exile in the Persian Empire. When the Spartans returned home, proper democracy was re-established in Athens with the introduction of major constitutional reforms created by Cleisthenes. The whole population of Athens was no longer divided into the four traditional tribes that had existed since the foundation of the city (named after the original Ionian tribal groups that had inhabited Athens), but was now divided into ten new tribes (named after famous Athenian heroes). The whole territory of Athens and Attica was divided into three districts (urban, countryside and coast), each of these being focused on a specific productive/economic activity (handicraft, agriculture and commerce), and each of the three districts was divided into ten parts (*demoi*), one for each of the new tribes (this way each tribe could comprise artisans, peasants and merchants). The number of archons was increased to ten and every year each tribe elected its own 'archont'. In addition to the archonts, each tribe elected one *strategos*, one of ten supreme military commanders that were to guide the Athenian military forces. The ten tribes also elected all the minor magistrates and thus were true electoral bodies. Finally, the Council of Four Hundred was renamed the *Boulé* and was expanded to 500 members (fifty for each tribe, chosen each year with a public draw). The *Boulé* was the only political body in Athens that could propose new laws, which would be later approved or not by the general assembly of all citizens. In addition, the *Boulé* controlled all the magistrates of the state, preserved the internal security of the city and was responsible for the foreign relations of Athens. It also controlled very strictly the finances of the state. The *Ekklesia*, the general assembly of all citizens, discussed all the issues related to the political life of the city during four meetings for each month. The *Areopagus* was not abolished, but was transformed into a purely formal assembly, having only ceremonial functions, especially religious ones, and was to be made up of all the ex-archons who had ended their period of service. From a military point of view, each of the ten tribes was to raise a *taxis* (regiment) of 1,000 hoplites and a *phyle* (squadron) of 100 cavalrymen. As a result, by the time of the Battle of Marathon in 490 BC, Athens could deploy an army with 10,000 hoplites and 1,000 cavalrymen.

Chapter 4

The Ionian Revolt and the Greco-Persian Wars

As we have seen, the western coast of Asia Minor had been progressively colonized by the Greeks, who created several new *poleis* in the region, assembled into two large communities, that of Aeolia and Ionia. Until 546 BC the Greek cities of Asia Minor flourished without problems, since they were not menaced by any bordering country, the interior of Anatolia being controlled by the Kingdom of Lydia, which had quite positive relations with the Greeks. Since 560 BC Lydia had been ruled by King Croesus, one of the richest monarchs of his time. At the beginning of his reign he reasserted Lydian dominance over Aeolia and Ionia, but this was only formal, the Greeks of Asia Minor being fully independent and only having to pay a yearly tribute in gold to Croesus. The Kingdom of Lydia, with the city of Sardes as its capital, was one of the most powerful of the Ancient World, but in 546 BC it was menaced by a new and enormous power appearing on the horizon: the Persian Empire. This, ruled by the new Achaemenid dynasty founded by Cyrus the Great, had conquered most of the Middle East after a series of brilliant and rapid military campaigns. Anatolia was the next target of the Persians, who could count on an immense multi-ethnic army mostly made up of light troops (both on foot and mounted). Croesus did not wait for the Persian invasion, but instead decided to attack first in 547 BC. At that time he was allied with Sparta, the Neo-Babylonian Empire and Egypt, so he had hopes of victory against the expanding Persians. After some inconclusive clashes in central Anatolia, the decisive battle took place in 546 BC at Thymbra. Croesus was soundly defeated and had to retreat to Sardes, which was soon besieged and then conquered by the advancing Persians. The defeated king was captured and his realm was absorbed into the Persian Empire. A few years later, in 539 BC, Cyrus also conquered Babylon to complete the military conquest of the Middle East. The Greeks of Aeolia and Ionia now bordered a gigantic empire, which had no intentions of preserving the previous privileges and liberties they enjoyed under Croesus.

Cyrus the Great soon organized an expedition against the Greek cities of Asia Minor, led by his Median general Harpagus. Although Harpagus was able to subdue the *poleis* of western Anatolia after a brief campaign, the Greeks had no intention of giving up the fight. They proved very difficult to rule for the Persians, refusing to pay taxes and being always ready to rise up in open revolt. In most areas of his growing

Greek *ekdromos* armed with *xiphos* short sword. (*Photo and copyright by Athenea Prómakhos*)

Greek hoplite employing his *kopis* slashing sword. (*Photo and copyright by Athenea Prómakhos*)

Duel between two hoplites, both armed with the *kopis* short sword. (*Photo and copyright by Athenea Prómakhos*)

empire, such as in Lydia, Cyrus the Great had formed an alliance with the various local aristocracies after defeating them, but such a political operation proved impossible for the Greek cities of Asia Minor, where all citizens had more or less the same rights and social position. The Persians were, for the first time, dealing with a people made up of free individuals and not of subjects, used to serve under a supreme monarch. The Achaemenids sponsored the ascendancy of tyrants in several *poleis*, but this was not enough to secure their control over Asia Minor. Most of these allied tyrants were quickly killed or expelled by popular revolts of their citizens. Most of the Greeks from Asia were sure that their mainland 'brothers' would help them against the foreign invader, since by the beginning of the fifth century BC western Anatolia was widely considered an organic part of the Greek world. The Persians were well aware of this, but had plans to continue their expansion towards Greece in the future. As a result, the Persians tried to form a network of alliances with some cities of mainland Greece. As we have seen, this plan partly worked with Athens, but the loyalty of Hippias to the Persian cause led to his removal as tyrant of the Athenians. While this happened in the Aegean, the Persians continued to expand in other areas of the Mediterranean; in particular, after the death of Cyrus the Great, they conquered Egypt. This event had a great importance from a military point of view, since after absorbing the Egyptians among their subjects the Achaemenids were able to count on large contingents of sailors and naval infantrymen. The Persians were used to the traditional warfare of Central Asia and had no experience of naval campaigns, but with the conquest of the Phoenicians and later the Egyptians, they were able to build an impressive fleet and could start planning an attack against Greece. In 499 BC a first expedition was mounted against the island of Naxos, organized by one of the tyrants loyal to Persia, Aristagoras of Miletus, but with the participation of a sizeable Persian military force.

The attack against Naxos, however, was a failure, as after a four-month siege the Persians abandoned the island, having suffered severe economic losses. They had underestimated the military capabilities of the Greeks and had shown a certain weakness, and before they could plan any further expansionist expeditions, their former Milesian allies, under the same Aristagoras, rose up in rebellion. This was the beginning of the Ionian Revolt, a conflict that would change forever the relations between the Greek world and the Persians. Several Greek cities of Asia Minor had already assembled their military forces in Myus, in order to support the Persian efforts against Naxos. However, when news of the Milesian revolt reached Myus, the Greek soldiers mutinied and joined the rebellion. Aristagoras presented himself as the leader of the Asian Greeks in the upcoming struggle and ordered the arrest of most of the other tyrants. In doing so, very rapidly, most of the Asian *poleis* became free from indirect Persian control and transformed themselves into democracies. Aristagoras was even able to capture the large fleet that the Persians assembled in order to attack Naxos, and as a result, the Achaemenids found themselves with no naval forces in the Aegean. The tyrants installed by the Persians had not been able to control the situation because, unlike those of mainland Greece, they were not popular leaders with great personal capabilities, just loyal officers who ruled on behalf of their Achaemenid masters. In the winter of 499 BC, in preparation for an anticipated Persian counter-attack by land and sea, Aristagoras went to mainland Greece in search of allies. Aristagoras tried to create an alliance with the Spartiates, but they refused, so he then went to Athens, since the city was already hostile to the Persians. After having been removed as tyrant of Athens, Hippias had become a member of the Achaemenid court and had been able to gain full support from his new protectors. As a result, in the years preceding the outbreak of the Ionian Revolt, the Persians had already ordered the Athenians to once again accept Hippias as their tyrant. The Athenians refused, and from that moment they considered themselves to be at war with the Persian Empire. Aristagoras, well aware of this, was able to gain unconditional support from the Athenians. The city of Athens, with its new form of democracy, had been a model for the *poleis* of Asia Minor in their struggle against tyrants imposed by the Persians. Furthermore, Athens was an Ionian city, like most of those that were now rebelling. Eretria also agreed to help Aristagoras, probably in exchange for the support received from Miletus during the long Lelantine War. The Athenians sent twenty of their trireme warships to Asia Minor, while the Eretrians sent a smaller contingent with just five triremes.

The Greek army of Asia, reinforced by the Athenians and Eretrians, assembled at Ephesus and then marched against the capital of the Persian province of Lydia. The Persians, taken by surprise, were not able to organize a proper defence, and after a brief assault, the Greeks conquered Sardes. The Persian garrison of the city, however, was not destroyed: under the command of Artaphernes, it still resisted in the citadel. During the siege of the citadel the lower city caught fire accidentally, which obliged the Persians to come out from the citadel in order to survive. Against all odds, their desperate counter-attack was successful and the Greeks retreated from Sardes. Most of the city, however, was destroyed. After this episode, the Persians understood that the revolt was a serious affair and thus started to assemble large military forces. Meanwhile the Greeks, demoralized by their setback, returned to their starting positions in Ephesus. Artaphernes organized a large cavalry force in central Anatolia, and with this was able to intercept the retreating Greeks on the outskirts of Ephesus. During the ensuing battle, the Greek army was routed and suffered high casualties. The remaining Athenians and Eretrians went back to their ships and retreated to mainland Greece. The Greeks of Asia, however, continued the revolt, as the Persians did not have a fleet in the area and could not deploy enough infantry to start besieging any of the rebel

Two lines of hoplites before being deployed in close formation. (*Photo and copyright by Athenea Prómakhos*)

cities. Due to this situation, the revolt spread to other Persian domains around the Aegean. The Greeks sent military expeditions against cities on the Hellespont and Dardanelles that were under Persian political influence, in order to assume control of those strategic areas. They also persuaded Caria and Cyprus to revolt against the Achaemenids, obliging the Persians to use part of their forces against these other rebelling provinces. Caria, located in south-western Anatolia, on the coast, was very near to Ionia and Aeolia and thus had long been influenced by the Greeks. Cyprus had experienced a very peculiar history after becoming independent from the Assyrians in 627 BC, the territory of the large island being divided into several small kingdoms that were heavily influenced by Greece but which later submitted to Egypt in 570 BC, albeit for a brief period.

Following the Persian conquest of Egypt, the Achaemenids also started to exert their influence over Cyprus. The conquerors, however, preferred not to occupy the island with a large military force but to permit the former small kingdoms to survive as semi-autonomous princedoms. Each Cypriot king was to act as a local governor and each kingdom had to pay a yearly tribute to the Persians. Like the Greeks of Asia Minor before 499 BC, however, the Cypriots were just waiting for the right moment to launch a rebellion against the Achaemenids. This opportunity came in 497 BC, when they decided to join the Greeks in their struggle. The Persians organized a large fleet to reconquer the island, mostly thanks to the help of the Phoenicians, long-time commercial rivals of the Cypriots. The rebels of Cyprus, however, asked for Greek

Two lines of hoplites protecting themselves with shields. (*Photo and copyright by Athenea Prómakhos*)

Two lines of hoplites with spears in the attack position. (*Photo and copyright by Athenea Prómakhos*)

help, and a fleet was sent to support them from Ionia. In the ensuing naval battle, the Greeks soundly defeated the Phoenician warships, but were unable to prevent the Persians from disembarking their land forces on the island. The Cypriots fought against the Persian expeditionary corps, but after a harsh battle they were routed. With no hope of success, the Greek fleet returned to Asia Minor and the Persians were gradually able to retake the whole of the island.

Meanwhile, the Achaemenids sent two smaller armies to the Hellespont and Dardanelles, where all the cities freed by the Greek rebels were besieged and reconquered. The Carians in the south, having assembled their military forces to face the Persians, were defeated during an initial clash, but received reinforcements from Miletus and thus continued to resist. Another Carian defeat soon followed, but in 496 BC they were able to organize an effective ambush against the main Persian force and thus temporarily gained the upper hand. At this point Aristagoras led an expedition into Thrace, probably with the intention of exploiting the great mineral resources of that region in order to support the revolt in Asia Minor. During this campaign, however, the great leader was killed and all his projects came to nothing. By 494 BC, the Persians had mustered large military forces in central Anatolia and were ready to launch a final offensive against the Greeks of Asia and Caria. A new Achaemenid fleet had also been assembled, whose presence was fundamental for supplying the land forces. The

Two lines of hoplites resting before or after battle. (*Photo and copyright by Athenea Prómakhos*)

Detail of a group of hoplites with their painted shields. (*Photo and copyright by Athenea Prómakhos*)

A group of hoplites in standing position. (*Photo and copyright by Athenea Prómakhos*)

Persian army moved directly against Miletus and besieged it, but the Greeks decided not to fight on land against the invaders and embarked their forces on all the warships they had available. The Greek fleet assembled at the island of Lade, near the coast of Miletus, and waited for the right moment to attack the Persian warships. In total the Greeks had 353 triremes, an impressive number for the time, but when the final naval clash took place they were decisively defeated, many of their warships changing side during the battle. After this decisive event, Miletus was stormed and destroyed by the Persian land forces. In south-western Anatolia some Carian strongholds continued to resist, but by 493 BC the great Ionian Revolt was practically over. The Persians even occupied the islands of Chios, Lesbos and Tenedos that had played an important part in the latter stages of the rebellion, and were now very near the borders of mainland Greece. Persian retaliation against the Greek cities of Asia Minor was terrible, but did not last long as the Achaemenids did not want to further damage the economic capabilities of such a rich region of their empire. Instead of restoring the old tyrants to power, they accepted the new democratic forms of government and even started to respect Greek customs without trying to modify them.

In 492 BC the Persians organized a European expedition, directed against Thrace, with the primary objective of subjugating the several tribes that inhabited the region. This was not the first European expedition of the Persians, as Darius I had already conducted a campaign against Scythia and Thrace in 513 BC. The Scythians, a strong nomadic people living in present-day Ukraine, had been allies of the Persians during the struggle against Babylon, but had then turned into a dangerous menace for the vast empire that the Achaemenids were building. As a result, hostilities began between the Persians and Scythians. Darius, wishing to eliminate these nomads once and for all, mounted an assault against their main European territories of southern Ukraine after crossing the Bosphorus Straits from Asia Minor, using a bridge of boats. While moving north, the Persians crossed Thrace and subdued, albeit temporarily, most of the local tribes. The Scythians used scorched earth tactics during the campaign and were thus able to retreat across the immense plains of Ukraine without fighting a single pitched battle against the Persians. In the end the expedition organized by Darius had no real winners, and ended with the retreat of the Achaemenids to their own territories.

After this Achaemenid foray, both the Scythians and Thracians returned to their previous independent condition. The Persians, however, started to consider those territories that they had temporarily conquered in 513 BC as part of their empire, and thus organized an expedition to 'reconquer' them in 492 BC. This was probably intended as a 'prodromic' operation, preparing the way for future offensives against Greece: the Persian army needed to have a base on the European continent. The Persian expeditionary corps of 492 BC was guided by Mardonius, son-in-law of Darius I, and departed from the Anatolia region of Cilicia (a vitally important territory which linked southern Anatolia with Syria, and thus the heart of the Persian Empire). The Persian army advanced by land to the Hellespont in northern Anatolia, marching along the coastline in order to retain direct contact with the fleet. At this point all the troops were embarked on the ships and crossed the Hellespont without particular problems. Once in Europe, the Persians focused on re-subjugating the Thracian tribes one by one. Since these tribes were politically divided, the occupation of southern Thrace was not a difficult task for Mardonius. By now the Persians had a solid base in Europe, but instead of moving north to fight against the Scythians, the Achaemenid Army moved west in order to enter northern Greece. The Persians soon reached Macedonia, at this time a semi-barbarous kingdom of little political and military importance. The Macedonians were under a mix of influences at the time, and thus their 'Greek' character was no stronger than their Illyrian or Thracian one. During the European expedition of Darius they had already recognized the Persians, albeit only formally, as their overlords; in 492 BC they did the same and thus Macedonia became a vassal state of the Persian Empire. Everything seemed to work well for Mardonius, but at this point of the campaign the Persian fleet was surprised by a terrible storm, which destroyed some 300 ships. The Persian navy had no proper knowledge of that part of the Aegean, and thus the disaster might have been avoided; in any case, the land forces were now left alone. Shortly after this event, the large Persian camp in Macedonia was attacked during the night by one of the strongest Thracian tribes, the Brygians, who had not yet been fully subjugated. This surprise assault caused serious losses to the Achaemenids and Mardonius was wounded. With hardly any fleet, he decided to retire to Asia Minor with all his forces, crossing the Hellespont using what remained of the fleet. Before going, however, the Persians crushed the Brygians and left some garrisons in Thrace and Macedonia.

Although the European campaign of Mardonius had only been a partial success, it had secured for the Persians the land approaches to the Greek mainland. In 491 BC, confident that the Greeks had been greatly impressed by his campaign in Thrace and Macedonia, the Persian Great King, Darius I, decided that the time had come to also annex mainland Greece to his immense empire. The Persians did not want to occupy the Greek cities with a large army, but simply wanted a formal submission from all the Greek *poleis*, as they had already done in Cyprus, for example. The 'surrender ceremony' required by the Achaemenids was very symbolic, including the offer of 'earth and water' from the new subjects to the Great King. Persian ambassadors were sent to all the major Greek cities demanding this ceremonial offer of submission, but in Athens the Achaemenid envoys were put on trial and then executed, while in Sparta they were simply thrown down a well. The Greek response to the Persian

Detail of different shield emblems. (*Photo and copyright by Athenea Prómakhos*)

Hoplites deployed in a *cuneus*, or wedge, attack formation. (*Photo and copyright by Athenea Prómakhos*)

Full heavy infantry panoply of a hoplite. (*Photo and copyright by Athenea Prómakhos*)

requests had been very clear. At this point, however, Sparta entered into a period of internal machinations due to a series of unexpected political events. The island of Aegina, unlike most of the other Greek communities, accepted Persian suzerainty. The Athenians, fearing that Aegina could be transformed into a new naval base for the Persians, asked the Spartans to intervene in order to deal with this problem. One of the two Spartan kings, Cleomenes, responded to the Athenian request for help and organized an expedition against Aegina. However, the other Spartan king, Demaratus, retracted his support for the military expedition and obliged Cleomenes to return. The latter, having been humiliated under the eyes of the Athenians, declared Demaratus a traitor and forced him to abandon Sparta. Demaratus went into exile to the Persian court, where he became one of Darius' personal advisors, like Hippias. Soon after these events, Cleomenes died unexpectedly; as a result, Sparta had to replace both kings in a very short time. Demaratus was replaced by his cousin Leotychides, while Leonidas took the place of Cleomenes. Meanwhile, the Athenians were able to submit Aegina, preventing the island from becoming an important naval base for the Persians.

After knowing of the political instability that was afflicting Sparta, the Persians decided to organize a military expedition against Greece in 490 BC. This was mostly intended as a punitive campaign of demonstration, in order to show all the Greek *poleis* that the Persian Empire was the most powerful state on earth. Athens and Eretria, the two cities that had directly supported the Ionian Revolt, were the main targets of the new Persian military force sent to Europe. This army was assembled in the heart of the Achaemenid Empire at Susa and then marched to the coast of Cilicia in Anatolia. Here the soldiers were embarked on a fleet that comprised 600 ships in total, a combination of warships and transport vessels, including those for horses. The Persian force advancing against Greece in 490 BC was not extremely large, because Darius did not want to permanently occupy any of the *poleis*: he just wanted to launch a demonstrative raid against Athens and Eretria, possibly destroying these two cities as an example for all the others. As a result, the ships transported roughly 25,000 warriors, of which only some 3,000 were cavalry. With these numbers the Persians could have easily defeated a single Greek city, but would have experienced serious difficulties in facing any Greek military coalition.

As usual with Achaemenid forces of this era, the army comprised a core of 'Persian' troops and contingents of auxiliaries from various areas of the empire. The Persian soldiers actually belonged to four different ethnic groups: Persians, Medes, Kissians and Saka. They provided the best infantry and most of the elite cavalry. While compared to the auxiliary contingents these Persians had heavier personal equipment, they were still lightly armed in comparison with the Greek hoplites. The auxiliaries were all armed as light infantry skirmishers and generally had little discipline to speak

Full hoplite panoply comprising a shield with scorpion emblem. (*Photo and copyright by Athenea Prómakhos*)

of: they were not particularly motivated and were forced to serve under the Persians, having been recently defeated and conquered by the Achaemenids. The Persian fleet landed some troops on the island of Naxos, which had repulsed an Achaemenid attack just before the outbreak of the Ionian Revolt. Most of the island's buildings were destroyed by the Persians, who enslaved a large portion of the inhabitants. Then the fleet moved against the island of Euboea to punish Eretria, with a large section of the army landing to besiege the city. The Eretrians remained inside the city walls rather than fight a pitched battle against an enemy with such superior numbers. After six days of attacks against the city walls, the Persians were finally able to break into Eretria and razed it to the ground. All the surviving inhabitants were enslaved and the city practically ceased to exist.

At this point the Achaemenid fleet headed south down the coast of Attica to the Bay of Marathon, where all 25,000 soldiers disembarked. The plain of Marathon was chosen by the Persians because it was quite near Athens (located just 25 miles north from the city) and was large enough to act as a base for their army. Hippias, the former

Hoplite panoply comprising bronze greaves. (*Photo and copyright by Athenea Prómakhos*)

Hoplite panoply with Chalcidian helmet and *kopis* sword. (*Photo and copyright by Athenea Prómakhos*)

tyrant of Athens, was with the Persian army, the Achaemenids intending to restore their 'advisor' as the supreme leader of Athens after punishing the city. It was Hippias, according to sources, who suggested the Bay of Marathon as a perfect landing place, as the Persians did not know the territory. The Athenians quickly assembled their whole army to face the invaders and sent 9,000 hoplites against the Persians, some 1,000 heavy infantrymen remaining in Athens to act as a garrison. The Athenians received no support from the nearby *poleis*, except for 1,000 hoplites sent by the small Boeotian city of Plataea. The latter, to escape from the Theban sphere of influence, had formed a strong military alliance with Athens some years before 490 BC. On one occasion the Athenians had already defended Plataea from an attempted Theban invasion, so the little city now felt duty-bound to support Athens against the Persian menace. The Greek army marched to Marathon and blocked the two exits from the plain, but the Athenians were too few to confront the Persians and preferred to wait for the arrival of other allied contingents. Philippides, Athens' greatest runner, was sent to Sparta to obtain military support. He arrived while the important religious festival of the

Carneia was taking place, so the Spartiates answered that their army would only move ten days later after the end of the religious rites. We simply do not know if the Spartiates decided to act in this way because of their religious zeal or because they wanted to see Athens destroyed by the Persians. Whatever the case, the Athenians received no help. After a stalemate of five days, and knowing that no further reinforcements were on the way, the Athenians decided to attack before the Persians made the first move.

The Greek hoplites advanced in perfect close order towards the enemy, marching at their usual slow pace. In the centre of the army the hoplites were arranged four ranks deep, while on the two wings they were deployed in a depth of eight ranks. It is clear that the Athenians wished to make a double envelopment of the enemy centre, with the Persians, having advanced against the Greek centre, heavily attacked from the flanks and the rear. When 200 metres from the enemy, before the Persian missiles could become effective against their ranks, the hoplites broke into a run and launched a devastating charge against the opposing infantry. The Achaemenid soldiers were taken completely by surprise, never having experienced close combat with an enemy bearing heavy equipment. Persian battles were usually fought from a distance, using missiles against enemies who, similar to themselves, wore little or no armour. During their charge, the Persian projectiles proved of little use against the armour and shields of the Greek hoplites. The Athenian wings quickly routed both the Persian flanks, where the auxiliary contingents were deployed, and while in the centre, thanks to their local superiority, the Persian contingents were able to hold the line for some time, they were finally encircled and crushed like the rest of their army. The defeated Persians fled in panic towards their ships, with the Greek hoplites in pursuit: the disorganized Achaemenid retreat soon turned into a rout, and the Athenians were even able to capture seven enemy ships before the Persian fleet could escape from the bay. When the battle was over Athens had been saved from destruction: the Greeks had lost just 200 men, while around 7,000 Persians were killed on the field. The ancient world had never seen such a demonstration of military superiority, but the game was not yet over for the Persians.

While the Battle of Marathon was just a small defeat in a far corner of the empire for the Persians, the Achaemenids could not tolerate the fact that a single Greek city had been able to thwart their military ambitions. As a result, they soon started to plan a second attack against Greece, but this time with a vastly superior military force. The Spartans, meanwhile, arrived on the battlefield of Marathon soon after the battle and were surprised by the Athenian victory: for the first time, they recognized the Athenians as fierce warriors. Athens had shown that not only the Spartiates could fight with courage. The balance of power was changing in Greece, but for the moment the Greeks had to prepare themselves for the anticipated return of the Persians.

Hoplite panoply with Attic helmet and *xiphos* sword. (*Photo and copyright by Athenea Prómakhos*)

Hoplite panoply with Chalcidian helmet and composite linothorax. (*Photo and copyright by Athenea Prómakhos*)

Hoplite panoply with Attic helmet and bronze greaves. (*Photo and copyright by Athenea Prómakhos*)

The decade from 490–480 BC was characterized by a series of important events which set the stage for the Second Greco-Persian War. Soon after Marathon, Darius I started to organize a new army for a second and more devastating attack against Greece. In 486 BC, however, Egypt rose up in revolt, so the Achaemenids had to use this new army in their African province. The Egyptian revolt proved very difficult to put down, forcing an indefinite postponement of the new expedition against the Greek *poleis*. In that same year Darius I died and the throne passed to his son, Xerxes I, who also inherited the difficult task of reconquering Egypt. After this was finally achieved, the Achaemenids resumed their preparations for the invasion of Europe. War materiel and provisions of every kind were stockpiled in great quantities, while tens of thousands of warriors were recruited from every province of the immense Persian Empire. Xerxes decided that his huge army would cross the Hellespont in order to reach Greece, instead of landing on the Greek coast, as his father had done in 490 BC. The Persians therefore built two new bridges of boats across the Hellespont, much larger and more solid than that which had been created for Darius' European campaign. The soldiers who made up Xerxes' army came from forty-six different ethnic groups and were all equipped according to their own military traditions. During the autumn of 481 BC these forces were mustered in Anatolia, where they underwent final preparations.

The number of soldiers who made up the Persian army has long been disputed, because Greek contemporary sources all give incredibly high numbers. Considering the manpower available to Xerxes and the strategic situation of all the areas of the Empire, it is reasonable to conclude that the Persian army invading Greece in 480 BC probably had a total of 200,000 soldiers. It was an impressive number for the standards of the time, especially compared with the meagre military resources of Greece. During subsequent operations the Achaemenid land forces would be supported by their fleet, since the army was to advance by marching along the coastline, receiving constant supplies and reinforcements from the ships. In total, the Persian navy deployed some 1,200 vessels (both warships and transports).

In the years following the Battle of Marathon, Athens witnessed the rise of Themistocles, a popular political leader who had the support of the lower social classes. Themistocles considered Marathon as the perfect starting point from which to build an Athenian naval empire to control the whole eastern Mediterranean. Having been voted into power, he started to use all the economic resources of his city to enlarge the Athenian fleet. With hundreds of triremes, the Athenians could repulse any Persian attack against Greece and defend their new commercial seaways. Athenian merchants dominated all the markets of the Aegean, while Athenian admirals exerted a strong political influence over all the coastal regions and islands of Greece. The naval programme launched by Themistocles was made possible by the unexpected discovery of a new seam of silver in the Athenian mines of Laurium: this silver was used to finance the construction of hundreds of new triremes, using the best materials that were available. By 480 BC Athens could deploy the best and largest fleet in Greece, comprising modern, well-made vessels. Themistocles' naval policy also had an important social consequence, since it permitted the permanent employment of thousands of *thetes* as rowers for the fleet. Themistocles was mostly supported by this social group, so such a move was made to augment the military importance of the *thetes*, who were not permitted to fight as hoplites in the land forces, which were dominated by the middle classes. In 481 BC, when it became clear that the Persians were preparing a new invasion of Greece, a congress of *poleis* was organized in Corinth to creating a defensive military alliance against the Achaemenids. Athens and Sparta played a prominent role in this meeting, putting aside, at least for the moment, their increasing rivalry. Of the over 700 Greek states that existed at this time, however, only 70 sent their representatives to the assembly at Corinth and joined the new alliance. Among the most important absentees were Argos and Thebes: the former, an enemy of Sparta, decided to remain neutral in order to await the defeat of the Spartiates; while the latter, an enemy of Athens, was ready to help the Persians if this would aid the consolidation of Theban hegemony over Boeotia.

Hoplite panoply with a Corinthian helmet and linothorax. (*Photo and copyright by Athenea Prómakhos*)

Hoplite panoply with *xiphos* sword and composite linothorax. (*Photo and copyright by Athenea Prómakhos*)

Hoplite panoply with Chalcidian helmet and composite linothorax. (*Photo and copyright by Athenea Prómakhos*)

In April 480 BC the Persian army, with the Xerxes in command, crossed the Hellespont and entered Thrace. Here the Achaemenids had already stored large amounts of food during the years that preceded the invasion, and had augmented these with the help of the local Thracian communities, which were now subjects of the Persian Empire. At this point there was another meeting of the Greek alliance, during which the Thessalians proposed to assemble an army and stop the Persians at the northern borders of Thessaly, the only flat region of Greece, where excellent war horses could be found and the local rulers could count on large cavalry armies. If conquered by the invading army, Thessaly would become the perfect base for the Achaemenids in Greece, where the numerous horses of Xerxes' army would find all the pasture they needed to survive, even during winter. The Greek assembly accepted the Thessalian proposal and sent an army of 10,000 hoplites to the Vale of Tempe in northern Thessaly. The Greeks did not have a precise idea of the enemy's numbers, but hoped to stop the Persians by defending a narrow mountain pass. Meanwhile, Xerxes entered the territory of Macedonia, where the local ruler, Alexander I, was a vassal of the Great King. The Macedonians did not put up any resistance, but passed some crucial information to the Greeks, informing them that the Vale of Tempe could be bypassed by at least two other mountain passes and that the Persian army was much bigger than expected. The Greeks therefore retreated, abandoning Thessaly. As a result, the Thessalians joined the advancing Persians and did not oppose the Achaemenid advance across their plains. The Greeks then decided to halt their retreat and attempt to defend another narrow mountain pass located north of Attica and Athens, where a small army of hoplites could try to stop Xerxes. The chosen place was known as the pass of Thermopylae and was the key to central and southern Greece, guarding the northern approaches to Athens, Thebes, Argos, Corinth and Sparta. The strategic importance of Thermopylae was huge, but not all the Greeks considered its defence as of primary importance: the Peloponnesian cities, including Sparta, preferred to organize a defence at the Isthmus of Corinth in order to protect their cities, but this would mean the destruction of Athens and Attica.

Hoplite panoply with Chalcidian helmet and linothorax. (*Photo and copyright by Athenea Prómakhos*)

Different models of Greek short swords: on the extreme left (top and bottom) are two examples of *xiphos*, while the two weapons with curved blades are of the *kopis* type. All the others are examples of the *machaira* sword, a longer variation of the *kopis* with a straight blade. (*Photo and copyright by Athenea Prómakhos*)

Different models of Greek helmets: on the top row are two Attic and two Chalcidian ones. Below are four Corinthian helmets and a single Chalcidian one. (*Photo and copyright by Athenea Prómakhos*)

Eventually, the strategic line supported by Leonidas of Sparta and Themistocles of Athens prevailed: the Greeks would send an army to Thermopylae, supported nearby by their fleet.

Leonidas faced strong opposition in his city, largely because the Persian attack happened during the important religious festival of the Carneia, as it had ten years before when the Persians disembarked at Marathon. The Spartiates would not move due to these religious restrictions and thus could not send their army to the pass at Thermopylae. Leonidas, however, had no intention of causing the destruction of Greece for such a petty reason, and thus marched with the 300 hoplites of his royal bodyguard to the pass. These men, the best of all the Spartiates, did not answer to the Spartan state but only to the king; as a result, the monarch could deploy them on any occasion and in any place. As with most of the elite Greek troops of the time, these 300 soldiers were probably mounted infantrymen, moving on horseback to travel long distances very quickly, but dismounting to fight as normal hoplites once the battlefield had been reached. Known as *Hippeis*, they were all veterans. Before their departure from Sparta, Leonidas gave orders to replace all the younger members of his bodyguard with experienced Spartiates who already had sons. This way the blood of the best Spartiates would not have been dispersed if all the *Hippeis* were killed in battle. The 300 chosen soldiers were accompanied by 900 servants, possibly Helots, with three for each hoplite. As a result, the Spartan force numbered 1,200 soldiers: 300 hoplite Spartiates and 900 Helots equipped as auxiliary light infantrymen. The small Spartan contingent was reinforced en route by troops sent from various *poleis* of the Peloponnese which had strong political links with Sparta. These numbered less than 3,000 and were made up of the following groups: 500 Mantineans, 500 Tegeans, 1,200 Arcadians, 400 Corinthians and 200 Phlians. With these 4,000 fighters, Leonidas reached the Thermopylae pass and started to organize a strong defensive position. He soon received a further 3,000 or so reinforcements from other Greek cities that had agreed to stop the Persians at the pass: 700 Thespians, 400 Thebans, 1,000 Phocians and 1,000 Locrians. As a result, Leonidas' army comprised a total of more or less 7,000 soldiers against the entire Persian army of Xerxes. After visiting Thermopylae, the Spartan king decided to camp at and defend the narrowest part of the pass. Known as the 'middle gate', this had already been fortified by the Phocians some time before with the construction of a defensive wall. Before the Persian arrival, Leonidas used his men to expand and reinforce the existing wall. The Spartans were informed by local people that the pass they were defending could be outflanked by an almost unknown mountain track, which had not been in use for a long time. Fearing that the Persians could find it, Leonidas sent the 1,000 Phocians to garrison the mountain track and guard the back of his army. When the vast Persian army arrived at Thermopylae, Xerxes understood that the Greek position was very strong and would be difficult to conquer. His immense army would be forced to fight in a very narrow pass, unable to deploy its great numerical superiority. The Great King sent an ambassador to Leonidas with peace proposals, but these were refused by the Greeks. The Persians then waited for four days before attacking, in the hope that the allies of the Spartans would abandon Leonidas after seeing the numbers of the Persian army. All the Greek contingents, however, held their positions, and thus the battle became inevitable.

At the beginning of the clash, Xerxes ordered an attack on the Greeks from distance with a contingent of 5,000 archers. The Persian missiles, however, caused no losses to the hoplites, who were well protected by their shields. At this point the Achaemenid monarch ordered a series of frontal assaults, with waves of 10,000 men. These were all repulsed by the Spartiates, since the Persians had no experience of close combat and had very little space for manoeuvre inside the pass. The Greeks rotated their contingents of hoplites in the front line and thus always had fresh soldiers facing the attackers, while the spears of the Persian infantrymen were too short to engage the hoplites. Before the first day of battle was over, Xerxes launched a final assault with the 10,000 chosen warriors of his royal guard, the famous Immortals, deadly warriors considered to be the best infantry of his army. However, even the Immortals were repelled, with very heavy losses. On the second day the Persians continued their frontal infantry assaults, but again with no success. Xerxes was then informed of the existence of the alternative mountain path flanking the Thermopylae pass. During the following night the Immortals were sent behind the Greek army, using the 'secret' path to encircle the defenders. At daybreak on the third day, the Immortals attacked the Phocians who were guarding the rear of the Greek army: the defenders retreated to a nearby hill and tried to resist, but could not stop the Persian advance.

At this point of the battle it was clear that the Greeks had been encircled and there was no hope of victory. Leonidas, as commander in chief, gave the possibility to retreat with honour to all his allies while he remained to defend the pass with his Spartiates. In the end most of the Greeks abandoned Leonidas, but not all: the Thespians and Thebans remained, as well as the servants of the Spartiates (who had no choice). By the time the Battle of Thermopylae took place, the city of Thebes had already joined the Persians, as had Macedonia and Thessaly, so the nature of the Theban hoplites who fought with Leonidas at the pass is not very clear. According to the few sources we have, these Thebans were not sent to fight against the Persians by their *polis* but were volunteers who decided to support the Greek cause and thus abandoned their home city. They were obviously among the many citizens in Thebes who were against the decision of forming an alliance with the Persians. This would also explain why they refused to abandon the field of battle when defeat seemed unavoidable for the

Greeks. Leonidas' last stand did not have only symbolic implications, but also some practical ones: thanks to his final resistance, more than 3,000 Greek allies were able to escape from the trap and thus continue the fight for the freedom of Greece. The last phase of the battle was terrible for both sides. Most of the hoplites were by now fighting with their swords, since the majority of the spears were broken. The Persians had a clear numerical superiority, but this did not prevent them from suffering terrible casualties. 10,000 Persians attacked the Spartiates from the front and another 20,000, including the Immortals, advanced from the rear. All the Greeks, including Leonidas, were killed after retreating to a small hill. Considering that 3,000 Greeks escaped from the battlefield before the final assault and that most of the Phocians in the rearguard were able to survive, Greek casualties amounted to around 3,000 men, including all the 1,200 Spartans. The Persians had more or less 20,000 warriors killed in just three days of battle for a narrow pass, amounting to 10 per cent of their total land forces. The route to the heart of Greece was now open for the invaders, but the Greeks still had important military resources to use in the struggle: the Spartan army and Athenian navy were still intact.

While these dramatic events took place on land, the combined fleet of the Greek *poleis* fought against the Persians at Cape Artemision. Themistocles supported the forces deployed at Thermopylae by guarding their flank exposed on the coast. He assembled the naval forces under his command at Cape Artemision, which held a very important strategic position, comparable to that of Thermopylae on land. The cape,

Detail of some Greek bronze helmets (three Corinthian and one Chalcidian). (*Photo and copyright by Athenea Prómakhos*)

Detail of some Greek bronze helmets (two Attic and two Chalcidian). (*Photo and copyright by Athenea Prómakhos*)

Nice examples of Greek bronze greaves. (*Photo and copyright by Athenea Prómakhos*)

not far from the narrow mountain pass, was located on the northern tip of Euboea. It dominated the only entrance to the small channel that divided Euboea from mainland Greece, and thus from Thermopylae. If the Persians entered this channel, Leonidas could have been attacked from the sea and the Persian navy could have landed troops in Attica. Themistocles' fleet included about 270 triremes, with 127 sent by Athens, forty by Corinth and the others by several different *poleis*, including ten from Sparta. The Greeks maintained their positions at Cape Artemision for three days, as did their land forces at Thermopylae pass. During the first day the Greeks repulsed a Persian assault and even launched an effective counter-attack, the waters of Cape Artemision proving too restricted for the immense Persian fleet, which struggled to manoeuvre. On the second day both sides reorganized their forces and there were no serious clashes, but the following day they fought with enormous courage and both suffered severe losses before returning to their starting positions at nightfall. While the Greeks had been able to resist for another day, it was by now clear that they had to change strategy. Themistocles, learning that Leonidas had been killed and Thermopylae had been taken by the Persians, had no choice but to evacuate Cape Artemision as soon as possible in order to defend Attica and the rest of Greece. The Greek fleet retreated to the island of Salamis, off the western coast of Attica and not far from Piraeus, the port of Athens. Since the Athenian army was embarked on the fleet and the Thebans had joined the Persians, there were no more Greek forces north of the Isthmus of Corinth that could defend Attica. As a result, the population of Athens was also embarked on the fleet and transported to Salamis. Meanwhile, Sparta and all the Peloponnesian cities, with the exception of Argos, started to prepare a strong defensive line on the Isthmus of Corinth, building a wall and demolishing roads.

During the following days Athens was occupied by the Persian army and completely destroyed: very little of the city remained, but most of the Athenians were alive and safe on the island of Salamis. Themistocles did not move from his position at Salamis but waited for the arrival of the Persian navy. His plan was desperate but simple: he wanted to fight another naval battle against the Persians, but this time in the narrow Straits of Salamis, where the great agility of the small Greek vessels would cause serious problems to the larger but less manoeuvrable warships of Xerxes. Against all odds, Themistocles' plan worked superbly. The Battle of Salamis ended in disaster for the Persians, who lost more than 200 warships and with them their naval superiority. By this point of the war the strategic situation of the two sides had changed considerably. The victorious Greek naval forces were now free to move across the Aegean and could have easily destroyed the bridges built by the Persians to cross the Hellespont, thereby isolating the invading land forces in Europe, with no possibility of retreating into Asia or receiving reinforcements. The Persian army in Greece was still very large and strong, but without the support of the fleet it would have experienced serious difficulties in crushing the Greek defences on the Isthmus of Corinth. If 7,000 hoplites had been able to defend the pass at Thermopylae for three days, the whole Spartan and Peloponnesian armies would have been able to stop the Persians at the isthmus for several months. Understanding the strategic situation, Xerxes decided to leave Greece with a substantial part of his army and cross the Hellespont before the Greeks could attack the bridges there. He left behind an army of some 80,000 chosen warriors, mostly Persians and Saka, under command of Mardonius. The numerical superiority of the Persians had now vanished, and the Greeks could start a counter-offensive to expel the foreigners from their lands. Mardonius retreated to Thessaly to reorganize his forces during the winter of 480–479 BC, while the remnants of the Persian fleet went to Samos, with no intention of once again facing Themistocles.

During the spring of 479 BC, after months of preparations, the Persians moved south again and advanced towards Athens, reoccupying the empty ruins of the city. This time, however, the Greeks assembled all their land forces to create a large single army, intending to fight a decisive pitched battle. The Spartan army crossed the Isthmus of Corinth and marched north of the Peloponnese, to free Attica, forcing Mardonius to retreat back to Boeotia, where he could count on the military support of Thebes and where the flat terrain was perfect to employ his powerful contingent of Persian cavalry. Mardonius ordered the construction of a large fortified camp at Plataea, north of the Esopus River in Boeotia, where he awaited the arrival of the Greek army with his 80,000

Three examples of composite linothorax (reinforced with bronze scales), one linothorax and a leather cuirass. (*Photo and copyright by Athenea Prómakhos*)

A selection of *hoplon* shields painted with different emblems. (*Photo and copyright by Athenea Prómakhos*)

Persians and 20,000 soldiers sent by Thebes and his other Greek allies, Boeotians, Thessalians and Macedonians. The Greek army, guided by the new Spartan regent Pausanias, comprised some 40,000 hoplites, with 10,000 Spartans, 8,000 Athenians, 5,000 Corinthians and 17,000 soldiers from other minor cities. When the Greeks arrived at Plataea, Mardonius launched a series of minor cavalry raids to lure Pausanias down to the plain located between the two armies, where Persian cavalry tactics could have been employed to full effect. During one of these raids, Mardonius' cavalry was

Photo showing the back of a *hoplon* round shield. (*Photo and copyright by Athenea Prómakhos*)

able to block the only source of water available to the Greek army, the Gargaphian Spring, as a result of which, after eight days, the Greeks fell back to a better position where fresh water was available. This difficult movement was conducted under cover of darkness, but its only result was to fragment the Greek battle line before sunrise, none of the contingents retreating at the same pace or following the same route. Mardonius, sensing an important opportunity, launched a general assault against the retreating Greeks, who were in complete disorder, with most of their groups being isolated and unable to support each other. The ensuing clash was a very confused battle, during which individual Greek contingents were able to repulse and then defeat the attacking Persians. The Spartans bore the brunt of the fighting and caused terrible losses to their opponents, while the Athenians also fought well, defeating the Theban phalanx after hours of violent, close-combat fighting. In the final phase of the battle the Greek army was able to break the Persian defences and destroy their camp, transforming Mardonius' retreat into a rout. The Persian army was practically destroyed, suffering 80,000 casualties, Mardonius being among the dead, while Greek losses amounted to just 1,500 men.

Meanwhile, in the Aegean, the remnants of the Persian navy had abandoned Samos and retreated to the Ionian coast of Asia Minor at Mycale. Here the Persians beached their ships and built a defensive palisade around them: they had no intention of fighting with the Greeks at sea again, and just wanted to preserve what remained of their fleet. The Greeks followed the Persians to Mycale and disembarked their soldiers to destroy the new enemy base. The Greeks had 40,000 men, but only some of them were hoplites, while the Persian force numbered 60,000, but again many of these were sailors and not soldiers. The Persian contingents from Asia Minor changed sides and joined the other Greeks during the ensuing clash, helping their former enemies in the final part of the battle. Some 40,000 Persians were killed and all the beached Achaemenid ships were destroyed, as well as the fortified camp of Mycale. The Persian navy no longer existed and the Greeks were now the masters of the Aegean and could return home, after checking with their own eyes that the Persians had destroyed the bridges across the Hellespont. The Second Persian Invasion of Greece had ended, but the war between the Greeks and the Persian Empire was not yet over. After Mycale, most of the Greeks wished to enter a new period of stability and peace, and did not want to continue fighting against the Achaemenids now that the Persian menace to their homes was over. But the Athenians had other ideas: although still rebuilding their own city, they had wider political ambitions. Now they had full control over the Aegean and could deploy the largest fleet in the Mediterranean, after the terrible sacrifices of 490–478 BC, they wanted to capitalize on their efforts and build a naval empire that could fill the vacuum left by the Persians. As a result, they continued to launch offensive operations against the last Persian strongholds resisting in the Aegean. The Chersonese, a peninsula on the southern coast of Thrace, was still in Persian hands: the Achaemenids continued to garrison the area, from their base of Sestos, because it was the place where the two bridges crossing the Hellespont had been built and where new bridges could be constructed for future invasions of Europe. After a difficult siege that lasted several months, the Athenian navy was able to sieze Sestos and capture all the materials that had been employed to build the Hellespont bridges. All the Persian garrisons of the Chersonese were captured or destroyed in the following weeks, thanks to the help of local Thracian tribes.

At this point the Greeks, who were still acting according to the terms of the alliance formed in 480 BC, decided to attack Cyprus. The Spartans, however, decided to leave the Hellenic Alliance and were soon followed by most of their Peloponnesian allies. It was now clear that the original anti-Persian military alliance was transforming itself into a naval coalition led by Athens, having as its main political objective substituting Persian influence over the eastern Aegean with an Athenian one. The Spartans, worried about Athens' ascendancy, had no intention of helping their own Greek allies to become even more powerful. After Sparta and other cities left the original alliance, the coalition changed name and became known as the Delian League, which was dominated by Athens since no other Greek *polis*, excepting Sparta, could deploy so powerful military resources. As a result, from 478 BC, the Delian League continued to fight against the Persians in every corner of the eastern Mediterranean, largely to expand the Athenian sphere of influence over Asia Minor. By forming the new military

Detail showing the back of a *hoplon* round shield. (*Photo and copyright by Athenea Prómakhos*)

The points of some Greek spears; the second from the right is of the kind usually employed by hoplites. (*Photo and copyright by Athenea Prómakhos*)

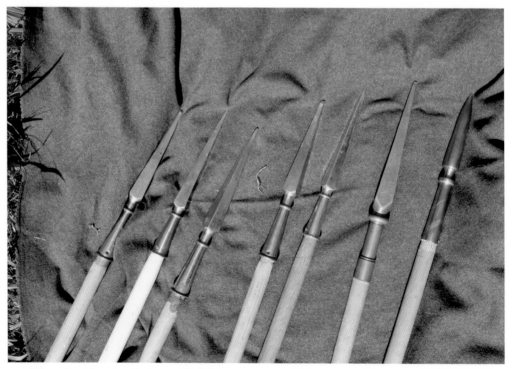

The spikes placed at the butt end of Greek spears. (*Photo and copyright by Athenea Prómakhos*)

alliance, the Athenians proposed a choice to all those cities that wished to became part of it: each member of the Delian League could either contribute to the military operations by sending soldiers and ships or could pay a tax that would be used to finance the Athenian war efforts. Most of the cities, tired of war, chose to pay the tax in exchange for Athenian military protection. Thanks to their victories in the Persian Wars, the Athenians had been able to become a great regional power to rival Sparta, thus forming a powerful alliance to counter-balance that of the Peloponnesian League created by Sparta. The first military action of the Delian League against the Persians was the attack on Cyprus in 478 BC. As we have seen, this large island had always been heavily influenced by Greek culture and was inhabited by a large number of Greeks, many of these being rich merchants or experienced artisans. As a result, together with Asia Minor, Cyprus had always been one of the Delian League's primary targets. The Athenians expelled the Persian garrisons and restored the formal independence of the local small kingdoms, which had to accept the suzerainty of the Delian League. As Cyprus was seen as an unimportant dominion of the Persian Empire, the Achaemenids did not make any serious attempt to reconquer it during the following decades.

The small kingdoms of Cyprus, however, did not readily accept Athenian 'protection', and revolted at least twice against the Delian League, in 460 BC and 451 BC. The second revolt was a major one, with the Athenians sending 140 warships to clamp down on it. Against the odds, however, the kingdoms of the island were able to resist and await the arrival of a Persian fleet to support their cause. The Achaemenids sent a large expeditionary corps, which joined forces with the rebels, and a decisive sea battle was fought in a location known as Salamis, the same name as the more well-known naval battle fought in 479 BC. The Athenians were also able to prevail this time, soundly defeating the Persian fleet. However, the Greeks realised that Cyprus was lost and that the only way to reconquer the island was to return with thousands of soldiers who could garrison it, which was something they could ill afford to do at that moment due to their involvement on other fronts.

In the years following 478 BC, the Delian League protected the new freedom of the Greek cities in Asia Minor, which had been freed after Mycale, and extended its influence over the coast of Thrace and in the Black Sea. In 469 BC the Persians assembled a large fleet at the mouth of the Eurymedon River in southern Anatolia, intending to use its warships to launch a major campaign against the Greek *poleis* of Asia Minor. After ten years of minor defeats, the Persians were slowly reorganizing themselves to face the Greeks again. The Delian League, however, aware of the Persian movements, attacked first before reinforcements could enlarge the enemy fleet at the Eurymedon River. The Persian warships, taken by surprise and unable to reach the open sea, were largely destroyed on the sandbanks of the river and their sailors fled before the Greeks

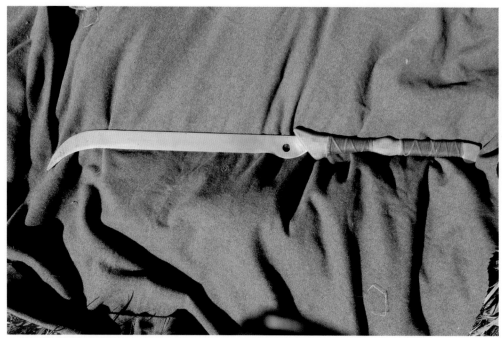

Example of Dacian *falx*, a terrible slashing weapon frequently also employed by the Thracians. (*Photo and copyright by Athenea Prómakhos*)

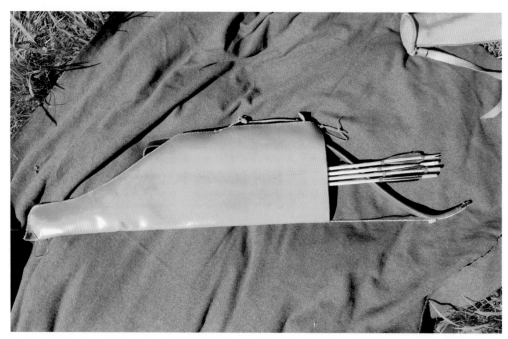

Quiver with arrows for a composite bow, of the same kind used by the Scythian archers in Athenian service. (*Photo and copyright by Athenea Prómakhos*)

Greek hoplite in full panoply, with 'muscle' cuirass of bronze and Corinthian helmet. (*Photo and copyright by Athenea Prómakhos*)

could disembark, joining a Persian army assembled nearby. The Athenians attacked the Persian camp and routed all the enemy forces they encountered, in a repetition of the Battle of Mycale. After re-embarking, the Greeks moved to the open sea and defeated the naval reinforcements, comprising 80 Phoenician warships, that the Persians had been awaiting at the Eurymedon River before returning to Greece. After such a severe defeat, the Persians were unable to send a fleet into the Mediterranean for decades, until 451 BC, when they tried to help the revolt of Cyprus against the Delian League. In addition, all Achaemenid plans for the reconquest of Asia Minor were cancelled.

In 460 BC, after the numerous pre-emptive strikes described above, the Athenians decided to adopt a much more offensive strategy in order to expel the Persians from much of the eastern Mediterranean. The Delian League's next objective was the province of Egypt, which had revolted against Persian rule on several occasions and was one of the last regions to be conquered by the Achaemenids. The last major Egyptian revolt in 486 BC had been crushed by the Persians, but the Athenians wished to cause a new uprising, massively supported by their fleet. An independent Egypt, allied with the Delian League, would have perfectly suited Athenian expansionist plans. In 461 BC a small revolt, probably instigated by the Athenians, started in Egypt. This was led by a local ruler named Inaros, who came from the Libyan desert bordering western Egypt. Once most of the country came under control of Inaros, after the expulsion of the Persian garrison, he formally requested the military help of the Delian League in view of the inevitable Achaemenid counter-offensive. The Athenians sent an impressive fleet with 200 warships, ready to help the Egyptians. The fleet had three main objectives: obtaining a naval base near the Nile Delta, gaining full access to the massive grain production of Egypt and restoring the traditional trading links existing between Greece and Egypt. When the Greeks arrived, the Persians were still blocking the Nile Delta with a small fleet of 50 Phoenician warships. The Athenians attacked and destroyed their opponents, sailing up the river and joining forces with the rebels. The Persians had already sent a large land army to reconquer their Egyptian province, and this was stationed not far from the Nile Delta. Once the Athenians disembarked their forces, Inaros felt strong enough to lead his combined Greek–Egyptian army against the Persians, and during the ensuing battle the Achaemenid troops were routed and suffered terrible losses. The few survivors retreated to the citadel of Memphis, where they were able to resist. The Greek-Egyptian army besieged Memphis for four years, but without success. In 455 BC, a new Persian expeditionary corps formed by elite troops invaded Egypt and defeated the besiegers of Memphis, after which the Greeks fell back to the island of Prosopitis in the Nile Delta, where their fleet was anchored. Here they were besieged by the Persians for 18 months, before the island was finally stormed and conquered by the Achaemenids, who dug canals to reach

Early example of Corinthian helmet, without crest. (*Photo and copyright by Athenea Prómakhos*)

Nice example of Illyrian helmet, having cheek pieces decorated with incisions reproducing a mouflon (wild sheep). (*Photo and copyright by Athenea Prómakhos*)

Prosopitis from the mainland. The Athenians suffered many casualties and only a few survivors were able to escape overland. The Egyptian revolt came to an end and a new Athenian squadron, arriving to reinforce Prosopitis when the island had already fallen, was also destroyed by the Persians, who attacked it from land and sea.

After the disaster of this Egyptian expedition, the Delian League decided to make peace with the Achaemenids. In 448 BC, with the Peace of Callias – named after the Athenian statesman who negotiated it – the long hostilities between the Greeks and Persians finally came to an end after nearly fifty years of war, lasting from 494–448 BC. The peace treaty was centred around four fundamental points: all the Greek cities of Asia Minor were to remain part of the Persian Empire but would enjoy a large degree of autonomy and be able to live by their own laws; Persian armies could not enter the western part of Anatolia, located west of the Halys River; Persian fleets could not sail along the western coast of Anatolia, Phaselis and the Cynaean Rocks being the last points they could reach respectively in southern and northern Anatolia; and the Delian League had to stop all military operations directed against Achaemenid dominions in

Chalcidian helmet with tall crest and a decorative mouflon sculpted in bronze. (*Photo and copyright by Athenea Prómakhos*)

the Aegean, notably Cyprus and Egypt. With the Peace of Callias, the Delian League transformed itself into an Athenian Empire, since there was no more external menace to fight but the Athenians continued to request money and military forces from their allies. As a result, Athens became the greatest naval power of the Mediterranean world. The Persians abandoned all their plans for future expansion towards Europe, but continued to counter Athens indirectly, working hard to create an alliance with Sparta in order to counter-balance the Athenian presence in the Aegean. A new phase of Greek history was beginning, with the Athenians and Spartans as protagonists, and the two great *poleis* fought each other in a terrible war of extermination.

Chapter 5

The Peloponnesian War and the Corinthian War

Around 450 BC Greece was the richest and politically most important area in the Mediterranean; the *poleis* had been able to stop the invasions of a real superpower and were now the dominant powers of the Aegean Sea. Athens and Sparta had gradually emerged, forming their own military alliances, with which they controlled most of the other Greek cities, either directly or indirectly. Athens ruled a naval empire based on international trade, while Sparta exerted complete control over the rich agriculture of the Peloponnese. Athens had the strongest navy in the world; Sparta had the strongest army. Athens was the land of democracy, while Sparta was ruled by the small and violent warrior caste of the Spartiates. The Athenians considered philosophy as the centre of a citizen's education; the Spartiates trained their young males every day in order to transform them into perfect warriors. Both cities had problems: the Athenians were gradually experiencing the degeneration of democracy, with the ascendancy of demagogues who threatened to destroy the established social order, while the Spartiates were under the constant menace of revolt from their Peloponnesian slaves, the poor but extremely numerous Helots. Both cities wanted to exert complete dominance over Greece, and to do so were gradually preparing for a major conflict with their rival. In 464 BC the Great Helot Revolt broke out in Sparta, causing serious difficulties for the Spartiates as thousands of slaves rebelled against their masters for the first time in more than a century. In clear difficulty, the Spartiates were obliged to ask for the help of their Greek allies in order to restore the social order of their communities. The revolt started after a terrible earthquake destroyed much of Sparta, providing the opportunity for the Helots to rise up with some hope of success. Many of the traditional Spartan allies sent their troops against the Helots, including Athens, but when 4,000 Athenian hoplites arrived the Spartans refused to receive their help and sent them back. All the other Greek contingents remained and helped to submit the Helots after extremely violent fighting.

While the Athenians were strongly offended by the Spartan decision, the Spartiates had feared that Athens had only sent the 4,000 hoplites to change sides and help the Helots. Once the rebellion was crushed, the alliance existing between Sparta and Athens, which had held since the time of the Persian Wars, was cancelled and a number of defeated Helots went into exile in Athenian territories. Diplomatic relations between the two cities became extremely tense. Athens signed treaties of military alliance with Thessaly and Argos, the latter being the traditional enemy of Sparta in the Peloponnese. The Athenians also concluded an important alliance with Megara, a former Spartan ally in the Peloponnese which was at war with Corinth, Sparta's main ally, for control of the Isthmus of Corinth and thus was in search of a powerful supporter. The Athenians wasted no time and took the opportunity to obtain a first foothold in the Peloponnese. War broke out between Athens and Corinth in 460 BC, while the Athenians were still fighting against the Persians. Athens was supported by Megara, while Corinth found an important ally in Aegina. After some Corinthian successes on land, Athens was able to prevail in all the major clashes of the war, whether on land or sea. Sparta remained neutral during the first phase of this war, but later decided to intervene in an indirect way. War had broken out between two allies of Athens, Phocis and Doris, and the Spartans sent an army to assist the latter city with the objective of transforming it into one of their allies. Phocis was defeated, but the Athenians sent a fleet to the Gulf of Corinth to stop the Spartan forces returning to the Peloponnese. Yet the Spartan army did not return home, but went into Boeotia,

Nice example of Chalcidian helmet. (*Photo and copyright by Athenea Prómakhos*)

Corinthian helmet having the surface of its top part sculpted in order to reproduce bronze scales. (*Photo and copyright by Athenea Prómakhos*)

The full panoply of an archaic hoplite, dating to around 600 BC. It comprises Corinthian helmet, bell cuirass, Argive shield, bronze greaves, short sword, shoulder guard and arm guard. (*Photo and copyright by Athenea Prómakhos*)

where the Spartiates concluded an alliance with Thebes and helped the city to defeat the other Boeotian *poleis*. As a result, Thebes became the undisputed dominant city of Boeotia and a new powerful ally of Sparta. At this point, feeling strong enough strong to make such a move, the Spartiates marched towards Attica against Athens, prompting the Athenians to muster all their land forces and those of their allies in order to stop the invasion. In total the Athenians could count on some 14,000 soldiers, including 1,000 hoplites sent by Argos, while the Spartans had 11,500 men, but only 1,500 of these were Spartiates, most of the others being their Peloponnesian allies. The two rivals clashed at the Battle of Tanagra in 457 BC, where losses were very heavy on both sides but the Spartans were eventually able to prevail.

After their victory the Spartan army was able to return home by crossing the Isthmus of Corinth, which had been abandoned by the Athenian fleet. The Athenians, however, had not been decisively defeated and were soon able to reorganize their forces to launch a campaign against Thebes. The Athenians found it unacceptable that their network of alliances in Boeotia had been replaced by a Theban hegemony imposed by the Spartans. At the subsequent Battle of Oenophyta, the Athenians defeated the Thebans and their Boeotian allies, after which Athens restored the situation in Boeotia and was able to concentrate all its forces against Aegina. Meanwhile, in Attica, the Athenians completed the construction of their famous 'Long Walls', which connected the city to the nearby port of Piraeus, forming a formidable defensive barrier in any future direct confrontations with Sparta. The Battle of Tanagra, fought on the border between Boeotia and Attica, had been an indecisive victory for the Spartiates. While they were able to take their army back to the Peloponnese, they were not able to attack Attica due to the serious losses suffered in the clash. After Oenophyta, the Athenians were able to occupy most of Boeotia except for Thebes and thus extended their political influence over another important area of Greece. In that same year, 457 BC, Aegina surrendered to the Athenians and became a member of the Delian League. Aegina's city walls were destroyed and all its warships were absorbed into Athens' navy. Phocis and Locris were invaded by the Athenians, who also sent a naval expedition against the coast of the Peloponnese in retaliation for the Spartan intervention against them. The Athenian warships circumnavigated the Peloponnese and ravaged its coasts, attacking and raiding the Spartan dockyards at Gythium. In the following months the Athenians landed a military force in the northern Peloponnese and defeated the city of Sicyon, which was allied to Sparta and Corinth, and meanwhile occupied the strategically important city of Chalcis in Euboea.

At this point of the war, when it seemed that the Athenians could do practically anything thanks to the massive superiority of their fleet, the Delian League was badly defeated in Egypt by the Persians and lost a large number of ships. As a result, hostilities came to an end and a truce was signed between the two warring coalitions, while the Athenians also made peace with the Persian Empire. In 449 BC, however, the truce came to an end when hostilities broke out between Phocis and Delphi: the latter city was dominated by Phocis and thus fought for independence. Phocis was by now an ally of Athens, while Delphi asked for Spartan military help. The Athenians sent an army to support Phocis and the revolt of Delphi was crushed. The events of 449 BC showed the Athenians, by now led by the great Pericles, how difficult it was to retain control over important regions such as Boeotia, Phocis and Lokris. Two years later, the Boeotian League, led by Thebes, revolted against Athenian rule and defeated a small Athenian force comprising 1,000 hoplites at the Battle of Coronea. With this clash the Boeotian League became independent from Athenian control, after ten years of foreign dominance. Pericles, understanding that something similar could happen in other regions dominated by the city, decided to abandon Phocis and Lokris. The Athenians were the masters of the sea, but had insufficient resources to control vast land regions of mainland Greece. Megara and Euboea then revolted against Athens, being sure that Sparta would support them. Pericles landed with an army in Euboea, but had to abandon military operations on the island because the Spartiates sent a

Cretan archer, equipped with sun hat and small round shield. (*Photo and copyright by Athenea Prómakhos*)

Scythian archer in Athenian service, wearing the traditional dress of his people. (*Photo and copyright by Athenea Prómakhos*)

A group of hoplites with an Iphicratean peltast (extreme left) and Thessalian light infantryman (in the centre, with the emblem of a boar painted on the shield). (*Photo and copyright by Athenea Prómakhos*)

large army against Attica with the intention of invading Athens. At this point, when it seemed that full-scale war was starting between Athens and Sparta, a new truce was signed between the two parties. The Athenians, benefiting from the truce, again sent their military forces against Euboea and finally submitted the island. In 445 BC, tired of war at least for the moment, Sparta and Athens signed the so-called 'Thirty Years' Peace', which included the following points: Megara was returned to the Peloponnesian League, Aegina became a tributary of Athens, all future disputes would be resolved with arbitrations and both parties agreed to respect the alliances of the other. The events starting in 460 BC and ending in 445 BC are commonly known by scholars as the First Peloponnesian War, which, unlike the subsequent and 'proper' Peloponnesian War, saw only limited fighting between Athens and Sparta. In any case, this conflict set the scene for the future and decisive confrontation.

Political stability only reigned in Greece for a few years, since in 433 BC the Athenians intervened in a local conflict between Corinth and Corcyra: the latter had been founded as a colony of Corinth, but was now growing as an important naval power and had revolted against the Corinthians. Athens decided to help Corcyra against Corinth and sent some warships, which were decisive in saving Corcyra from complete destruction. After this, at the request of the Corinthians, the Spartiates summoned all the members of the Peloponnesian League to Sparta in 432 BC. The Corinthians threatened to leave the Peloponnesian League if the Spartiates did not organize a strong reaction against the Athenians. They felt Athens had not respected the terms of the peace treaty signed in 445 BC, and thus had to be punished before Peloponnesian interests could be damaged any further. The Spartiates decided that the time had come for a final confrontation against Athens, and thus the Peloponnesian League declared war on the Delian League. During the first phase of the Peloponnesian War, known as the Archidamian War (431–421 BC), the Spartans soon invaded Attica and ravaged the countryside surrounding Athens. However, the city and the port of Piraeus, thanks to the existence of the Long Walls, were able to resist and continue receiving supplies from every corner of the Athenian Empire. In addition, the Spartans could never remain in Attica and occupy it for periods longer than forty days, as the hoplites of their allied contingents had to return home every three weeks to work as peasants and the Spartiates always had to keep an eye on the Helots working on their farms. Pericles feared a pitched battle against the Spartans, whose land forces were much more numerous than the Athenian ones, but this apparently passive conduct had as its main objective the consuming of the limited economic resources of the Peloponnesian League.

While these events took place on land, the Athenian navy was able to win some minor clashes against the inferior naval forces of the Peloponnesian allies. In 430 BC, however, the 'Plague of Athens' changed the course of the war, with many thousands of citizens, packed in the city because of the Spartan offensives, dying after terrible sufferings. Half of the Athenian population died, including Pericles, drastically reducing their available manpower. Fearing that the invading soldiers could also be killed by the plague, the Peloponnesian League army retreated from Attica. After Pericles' death, the Athenian leaders adopted a much more aggressive strategy, augmenting the number of naval raids launched against the coasts of the Peloponnese and creating an important naval base on the small island of Sphacteria, located at the entrance to the bay of Pylos in the Peloponnese. The base at Sphacteria soon started to be used by the Athenians as a centre of coordination for their raids against the Peloponnese. Thanks to their presence on the island, they could also start supporting the Helots in view of a possible general uprising against the Spartiates. In 425 BC the Athenian forces based on Sphacteria won an important naval battle against the Spartans at the Pylos Peninsula, after which 400 Spartiates remained isolated on Sphacteria and 100 of them were killed during subsequent fighting. The remaining 300 were captured and sent to Athens as hostages. This defeat, albeit small for Sparta, had great symbolic significance: for the first time, Spartan hoplites had been captured in large numbers after a humiliating defeat.

Since the Athenian war effort was mostly made possible due to the large amounts of silver extracted from the mines at Amphipolis, an Athenian colony in Thrace, the

Iphicratean peltast, equipped with Chalcidian helmet and armed with kopis sword in addition to his javelins. He is still using a traditional pelte shield instead of the new oval one and wears a couple of bronze greaves. (*Photo and copyright by Athenea Prómakhos*)

A line of Greek hoplites, supported by a Thracian peltast on the right (with his full national costume and equipment). (*Photo and copyright by Athenea Prómakhos*)

Spartans decided to organize an expedition against the mining centre. The Spartans easily captured Amphipolis after marching across Greece for hundreds of miles. The Athenians attempted to reconquer their colony in 422 BC, but were repulsed and utterly defeated by the Spartan garrison. In 421 BC the Peace of Nicias ended the first phase of the Peloponnesian War, under which the Spartans gave back Amphipolis to Athens in exchange for the 300 hoplites captured at Sphacteria several years before. The peace, however, only lasted for six years, since both sides were ready to resume hostilities as soon as possible. During the short-lived peace the Athenians encouraged Argos to organize an anti-Spartan coalition in the Peloponnese, which would have comprised all the democratic cities of the region. In 418 BC Argos, Mantinea and several Arcadian cities united their military forces against the Peloponnesian League, supported by a small Athenian expeditionary force under the new Athenian leader, the demagogue Alcibiades. At the Battle of Mantinea in 418 BC, the Spartans and their Tegean allies soundly defeated the Argive alliance. After this clash Sparta regained dominance over the Peloponnese and the few surviving Athenians were expelled from the region, while Argos changed sides and abandoned its democratic institutions. Mantinea and all the Arcadian cities were also forced to rejoin the Peloponnesian League. A new and decisive phase of the conflict was now starting.

Thracian peltast, with the peculiar cap and boots worn by Thracian warriors. Note the characteristic badge painted on the *pelte* shield, comprising two eyes. (*Photo and copyright by Athenea Prómakhos*)

At this point of the war, it became clear that the Spartans did not have enough resources to conquer Athens, but the Athenians were not strong enough to menace the Spartan hegemony over the Peloponnese. As a result, Alcibiades started to plan a large expedition outside Greece with the objective of conquering new resource-rich territories full of gold and silver, which were badly needed to continue the war, but also grain. At that time Sicily was probably the richest and most flourishing region of the whole Greek world, an island covered with large *poleis* and containing many natural resources. The most important city of Sicily, dominating most of the others, was Syracuse, a colony of Corinth and thus favourable to the Peloponnesian League. Syracuse had become the leading centre of Sicily thanks to the wars fought by the Greeks of Sicily against the Carthaginians, who had occupied most of western Sicily around the time of the Persian Wars and had ambitions of conquering the whole island. Syracuse, with an alliance made up of all the Sicilian Greeks, had been able to defeat the Carthaginians, halting their advance. As a result, by the time Alcibiades decided to attack Sicily, Syracuse had a size and population that were comparable to those of Athens. Differently from the armies of mainland Greece, that deployed by Syracuse comprised large cavalry contingents rather than mainly hoplite infantry. Defeating Syracuse would be the first step towards the Athenian conquest of Sicily. The Athenian contingent sent to the island, however, was too small: just 100 warships with around 5,000 soldiers. Athens had already sent some soldiers to Sicily in 427 BC to operate against Syracuse, but these had seen little combat and caused no serious damage to the enemy. With the arrival of the new expedition, the number of Athenians in Sicily was increased, but not enough to represent a serious threat for Syracuse.

The beginning of the Sicilian campaign was quite positive for the Athenians, since the newcomers were joined by the forces of several local cities that opposed Syracusan hegemony over the island. Few military operations took place during the first months of the campaign, and during the winter of 415/416 BC the Athenians retreated to their quarters on the island. Alcibiades, who had planned the Sicilian campaign from the beginning, was substituted by a new commander, Nicias, for political reasons, and thus the Athenians did not have a clear idea of how to continue their operations in Sicily. Meanwhile, Sparta sent a contingent of 1,000 soldiers to support Syracuse, along with an experienced military commander, Gylippus, who assumed overall command of all the anti-Athenian forces in Sicily. In subsequent months the Athenians were defeated in several small clashes and were pushed back from Syracuse. Most of the initial support received from local *poleis* vanished, while the allies of Syracuse sent strong contingents to support Gylippus. At this point Athens sent another 5,000 hoplites and some light troops as reinforcements, but they could not change the situation, and after several further defeats the Athenian commanders decided to abandon Sicily in order to avoid

Greek hoplites in battle formation. (*Photo and copyright by Athenea Prómakhos*)

Greek hoplites advancing in close order. (*Photo and copyright by Athenea Prómakhos*)

Greek hoplite with Corinthian helmet and composite linothorax. (*Photo and copyright by Athenea Prómakhos*)

complete destruction of their forces. However, the journey back to mainland Greece was postponed due to bad omens (a lunar eclipse). This delay forced the Athenians to fight a decisive naval clash against the Syracusan triremes in the Great Harbour of Syracuse, during which most of the Athenian fleet was destroyed. Completely isolated, the Athenian land forces had no choice but to move inland in order to find support from local cities. But the Athenian retreat from the outskirts of Syracuse, soon became a rout, the hoplites attacked by the superior Syracusan cavalry, which inflicted terrible losses. All the remaining Athenians were killed or captured: the prisoners of war were enslaved and sent to work in the Syracusan mines. The Sicilian campaign had been a total failure, causing significant human and material losses to Athens, and was a real turning point in the Peloponnesian War.

While these events took place in Sicily, in Greece the Spartans built a fortified position near Athens at Decelea, thanks to which they were finally able to have a permanent military presence in Attica for the entire duration of a year, thereby greatly damaging the agriculture of the region with frequent raids. In addition, the Spartans were able to occupy the Athenian silver mines and freed more than 20,000 slaves 'working' for Athens. Due to these events, the Athenians started to suffer from a terrible lack of food and funds. Most of Athens' allies rose up in open revolt, especially in Asia Minor. The Syracusans sent a new fleet to the Peloponnese to support Sparta, while the Persian Empire started to support the Spartiates by sending large amounts of money and numerous warships. Gradually, Sparta started to construct a fleet comparable in size and quality to the Athenian one. All the old enemies of Athens were now fighting together to destroy the Athenian Empire once and for all.

In 411 BC, since it was clear that Athens was going to lose the war, 400 oligarchs of the city staged a revolt against the democratic government and tried to install a pro-Spartan government. The Athenian navy, however, opposed the coup and moved from the island of Samos with its remaining 100 warships. The Athenian sailors elected Alcibiades as their supreme commander and were able to restore democracy in the city after a short period. In addition, during 410 BC the Athenian fleet was able to inflict a serious defeat on the expanding Spartan navy at the Battle of Cyzicus. Meanwhile, after forming an alliance with Sparta, the Achaemenids had launched a campaign of reconquest against the Greek *poleis* of Asia Minor that ended with a decisive Persian victory. In 406 BC Alcibiades was again removed from his role as supreme commander of Athenian military forces, for political reasons, as a result of which the Spartans felt strong enough to engage the Athenians in a major naval clash. This engagement, known as the Battle of Arginusae, ended with a great victory for Athens: while the Spartan navy was improving, it had not yet reached the same level as its Athenian counterpart. By now the military leadership of Sparta was in the hands of Lysander,

Detail of Corinthian helmet with tall crest. (*Photo and copyright by Athenea Prómakhos*)

Full heavy panoply of an archaic hoplite, including bell cuirass and leg guards. All the bronze armour is heavily sculpted. (*Photo and copyright by Athenea Prómakhos*)

Greek *psilos* light infantryman, throwing a stone; note the practice of wearing an animal skin on the left arm. (*Photo and copyright by Athenea Prómakhos*)

a highly experienced and intelligent naval commander. After the Battle of Arginusae, Lysander planned an ambitious attack against the Athenian bases in the Dardanelles in order to block the vast amounts of grain reaching Athens from the Black Sea, now the main source of food for the city, since Attica was under constant threat from the Spartans. The Athenians had no choice but to send all their remaining warships against Lysander's superior fleet in the Dardanelles. In 405 BC, at Aegospotami, the decisive clash of the Peloponnesian War was fought. For the first time, the Athenian navy was completely destroyed, suffering the loss of 168 vessels. With no more fleet, the Athenians could not continue their resistance against Sparta. Later the same year, Athens surrendered and the conflict came to an end: the city had to demolish its walls, give up its powerful navy and cede all its overseas territorial possessions. The main allies of Sparta – Corinth and Thebes – proposed the destruction of the city of Athens and the enslaving of all the surviving inhabitants. The Spartiates, however, refused their demand, and instead obliged Athens to enter into the Spartan system of political alliances as a vassal state. Democracy was suspended and a pro-Spartan oligarchic government was installed in Athens, known as the government of the 'Thirty Tyrants'. In 403 BC, however, a popular revolt soon restored democracy in Athens.

In the years following the end of the Peloponnesian War, the relationship between the Spartiates and their main allies, Corinth and Thebes, started to deteriorate. Sparta had suffered little during the war in comparison to its allies, who had meanwhile received practically nothing from the spoils of the Athenian Empire. All the economic tributes previously received by Athens were now collected by Sparta, which now exerted almost complete dominance over mainland Greece. This situation was unacceptable for Corinth and Thebes, two *poleis* with great political ambitions for their future. In 398 BC the Spartan army mounted an expedition against the Persians in Asia Minor, wishing to liberate the Greek cities of the region and to absorb them into the new Spartan Empire. Under the command of King Agesilaus, the Spartans obtained a string of victories over the Achaemenids and freed a large part of Asia Minor. Fearing a permanent Spartan presence in Anatolia, the Persians encouraged Corinth and Thebes to rise up against Sparta in mainland Greece, forcing Agesilaus to abandon Asia Minor in order to restore Spartan hegemony over Greece. The Persian plans worked perfectly and the Spartans abandoned Asia Minor. In addition, the anti-Spartan alliance sponsored by the Persians was joined by two historical enemies of the Spartiates: Athens and Argos. For the first time Sparta was alone against the other four major Greek cities: Corinth, Thebes, Athens and Argos. The new conflict, known as the Corinthian War, started in 395 BC with the Theban invasion of Phocis, an ally of Sparta. The Spartiates responded by sending two armies against Boeotia, but one of these was severely defeated before joining forces with the other. As a result of this early setback, many ex-Spartan allies joined the anti-Spartan alliance. Most of the Greek *poleis* had never accepted Sparta's permanent dominance over mainland Greece. The new allies – Thebes, Corinth, Athens and Argos – assembled a large army at Corinth and marched against Sparta. The two armies clashed in a major pitched battle at Nemea, in the Peloponnese, where 24,000 hoplites of the allies were soundly defeated by 18,000 Spartans.

Meanwhile, the Persians had assembled a large fleet that started to operate against the Spartans. After conquering Rhodes, the Persian navy fought the Spartan fleet at Cnidus, off the coast of Asia Minor. The Spartans were utterly defeated and lost most of their precious warships. As a result, the Persian navy could turn its attention against the new Spartan bases in Asia Minor, conquering most of them one by one. The Spartan navy had been wiped out in a single battle and no longer represented a serious menace for Sparta's enemies in the Aegean. Before the Persian naval victory, Agesilaus had already started his retreat from Asia Minor: since the Spartan navy now did not control the sea routes, Agesilaus marched back to Greece by land after crossing the Hellespont. He crossed Thrace, Macedonia and Thessaly, the Spartans being attacked in the latter region. Upon reaching the borders of Boeotia in 394 BC, they were also forced to fight against the Theban army at the Battle of Coronea. Agesilaus was victorious and thus could finally reach Sparta after a long and arduous journey.

The strategic situation of the war was clear: the Spartans were masters of mainland Greece, but could not exert any control at sea. Thanks to Persian funds, the Corinthians were able to rebuild and enlarge their fleet, while the Athenians could rebuild their city's fabled walls. At this point, however, a civil war broke out in Corinth, fought between the democratic faction (supported by Argos) and the oligarchic one (backed by Sparta). The democratic faction was able to prevail in the city, but the oligarchic exiles seized Lechaeum, Corinth's port on the Gulf of Corinth, with Spartan help. The allies sent a military force against Lechaeum, but were repulsed by the Spartan army that advanced into the northern Peloponnese. Peace talks then took place, but came to nothing. The Persians, realising that thanks to their help the Athenians were gradually rebuilding their old naval empire, secretly changed sides, starting to support the Spartans with money and ships. In 391 BC Agesilaus campaigned around Corinth, hoping to conquer the city with his forces, but after some initial success he was soundly defeated at the Battle of Lechaeum by an Athenian force commanded by Iphicrates, who was able, for the first time, to defeat the Spartiates using hit-and-run light infantry tactics. After this defeat, Agesilaus returned to Sparta while the Athenians continued to campaign around Corinth. Soon after these events, Argos and Corinth decided to form a single state and thus merged their citizens, albeit temporarily. During the final years of the Corinthian War only minor actions took place on land, while at sea the Spartans were partly able to recover and cause some damage to the Athenians, capturing a number of their merchant ships and raiding the port of Piraeus. In 387 BC the conflict finally came to an end with the Peace of Antalcidas, also known as the 'King's Peace' because it was strongly sponsored by the Achaemenid monarch. The political situation returned to the status quo, except for the fact that Asia Minor was reconquered by the Persians: Sparta remained the prominent military power of Greece, albeit quite weakened; Thebes relinquished to the role of leader of the Boeotian League; Argos and Corinth were separated, the latter being readmitted into the Peloponnesian League; and Athens acquired some small territories in the Aegean and continued to exert a certain influence at sea.

Greek *psilos* light skirmisher, armed with a simple stone. (*Photo and copyright by Athenea Prómakhos*)

Greek *psilos* wearing Thessalian sun hat and armed with light javelins. (*Photo and copyright by Athenea Prómakhos*)

Thessalian officer, with the characteristic sun hat and cloak worn by Thessalian cavalry. (*Photo and copyright by Athenea Prómakhos*)

Chapter 6

The Theban-Spartan War and the Rise of Macedonia

After the end of the Corinthian War, Thebes was in a new political position for several reasons: Athens, defeated in the Peloponnesian War, was focusing on the restoration of a naval empire instead of exerting influence over mainland Greece; Sparta, despite winning the Corinthian War, was experiencing the first phase of a crisis essentially caused by the lack of Spartiate manpower; and Argos and Corinth had not been able to form a single state and were both greatly inferior to Sparta in the Peloponnese. As a result, there were all the conditions necessary for a Theban military ascendancy. The Thebans had long dreamed of acquiring political prominence over all the rich cities of Boeotia and becoming a great land power. During the previous decades, as we have seen, they had only been able to dominate the Boeotian League for brief periods, and their expansionist ambitions had always been countered by the nearby city of Athens. After the Corinthian War, understanding that the Thebans would soon resume their usual expansionist projects, the Spartans decided to strike first, occupying the citadel of Thebes in 382 BC and installing a pro-Spartan government in the city. The surprise move left the Theban democrats with no option but to abandon their city and flee to Athens as political exiles. Here they reorganized under the charismatic leadership of Pelopidas and gained the support of the Athenian government. In 379 BC, after three years of preparation, Pelopidas' exiles marched on their city with the support of a small Athenian military force, managing to expel the Spartan garrison and the pro-Sparta government thanks to the decisive help received from opposition within the city. The latter were guided by Epaminondas and Gorgidas, two young leaders who had gradually organized a clandestine army in preparation for a general revolt. After expelling the Spartans, the new Theban government formed an alliance with Athens to help them resist the expected Spartan response. This duly came in 378 BC, when the Spartan monarch Agesilaus II launched an invasion of Boeotia. The attacking force assembled by the Peloponnesian League was impressive, numbering around 30,000 soldiers. Facing them were 13,500 Theban troops who received some support from Athens, but this consisted of just 5,200 men, a good number of whom were mercenaries and not citizen-soldiers. The invaders were able to ravage the countryside after breaking the initial Theban defences. The two armies then faced each other on the field of battle, but there was no clash of arms. Agesilaus, understanding that his enemies would have fought until death and that his forces were in no condition to besiege Thebes after enduring a major pitched clash, decided to abandon Boeotia and retreated with his Spartan army.

A small Spartan garrison was left in the allied Boeotian city of Thespiae, from where the Spartiates were able to launch raids against Theban territory while their enemies did the same against Thespian lands. It was clear, however, that sooner or later a decisive clash would come between Sparta and Thebes. The Thebans were eventually able to defeat the Spartan garrison at Thespiae and killed the supreme Spartiate commander in the area, but the Spartans continued to have a presence in Thespiae. A second expedition against Thebes by Agesilaus ended in failure like the previous one, the Spartan army again abandoning Boeotia after only fighting a series of skirmishes. The Spartans clearly needed a decisive victory over the Thebans as

Greek *psilos* light infantry skirmisher. (*Photo and copyright by Athenea Prómakhos*)

Greek light infantryman with Chalcidian helmet and round shield. (*Photo and copyright by Athenea Prómakhos*)

Greek light infantryman throwing his javelins. (*Photo and copyright by Athenea Prómakhos*)

soon as possible or they would lose their hard-earned military reputation forever. The Spartans still had considerable military forces garrisoning cities in Boeotia, a situation that proved unacceptable for Thebes. In 375 BC, a small Theban raiding force fought a pitched battle against one of the Spartan garrisons at Tegyra, with 500 Thebans (300 elite hoplites of the famed Sacred Band and 200 cavalrymen) facing 1,000 hoplites of two Spartiate regiments. Against all odds, it resulted in a clear Theban victory, the Spartans suffering heavy casualties after failing to encircle the enemy. While the Battle of Tegyra was just a minor defeat for Sparta, it showed to the Greek world for the first time that Thebes could deploy a hoplite unit possessing training and morale comparable to those of the 'invincible' Spartiates.

Following Tegyra, the Thebans launched a series of attacks against the other Boeotian *poleis* that were still loyal to Sparta: Thespiae, Tanagra and Plataea were subjugated, and the Theban-led Boeotian League was formally re-established. What

Greek light infantryman armed with *xiphos* short sword. (*Photo and copyright by Athenea Prómakhos*)

Greek hoplite with the emblem of an owl painted on his shield; this animal was one of Athena's symbols and thus one of the most popular shield emblems among Athenian hoplites. (*Photo and copyright by Athenea Prómakhos*)

Greek hoplite with Chalcidian helmet and composite linothorax. (*Photo and copyright by Athenea Prómakhos*)

the Spartans had tried to avoid after the Corinthian War was now becoming reality. The new Boeotian League had a democratic character, with a federation guided by an executive body made up of seven generals (*Boetarchs*), each elected by one of the seven territories into which Boeotia was divided. For the first time in their history, all the Boeotians understood that the real enemy was Sparta and not Thebes. Thanks to the introduction of democracy in the League, a newfound solidarity started to pervade the region and soon the terms 'Theban' and 'Boeotian' started to be used interchangeably. At this point, seeing that Thebes was rising to prominence over mainland Greece, Athens changed its political attitude and started to covertly support the Spartans. During the following years the Spartans invaded Boeotia on several occasions and raided the countryside around Thebes, but they never engaged in a proper pitched battle against the Thebans. The Thebans, well aware of their own power, were just waiting for the right moment to confront the Spartiates under the most favourable conditions.

In 371 BC, after the failure of peace talks sponsored by Athens, both Sparta and Thebes prepared for war. The decisive clash of the new conflict was fought at Leuctra, where 6,000 Boeotians crushed a Spartan force of some 10,000 soldiers (only 700 of whom were elite Spartiates). While Epaminondas was in overall command of the Boeotian Army, Pelopidas led the Sacred Band. During the clash, one of the most famous in the military history of Ancient Greece, Epaminondas employed some incredibly innovative tactics that were decisive in securing victory. The traditional phalanx formation of the Greek hoplites had a natural tendency to veer to the right during battles, because it was normal for each hoplite to seek shelter for his unarmed side with the shield of the fighter located to his right. As a result of this tendency, Greek military commanders always placed their best troops on the right flank of their armies. At Leuctra, for example, the Spartan commander placed his 700 Spartiates on the right. Epaminondas, however, did something completely different, since he had to fight a much more numerous enemy and thus risked being outflanked. Firstly, he took the best troops of his army, including the Sacred Band, and deployed them on his left flank in order to face the Spartiates, arranging them in a much more dense formation, fifty ranks deep instead of the usual eight to twelve ranks. As a result, the Thebans not only had their best troops on the left but also enjoyed a local numerical superiority over the elite Spartiates. Secondly, Epaminondas adopted, for the first time in recorded history, an oblique formation. Since his right flank was now formed by troops of mediocre quality and inferior in numbers to the enemies confronting them, he instructed his hoplites there to avoid battle with the enemy and withdraw gradually as the Spartans advanced. In that sector the Spartan line was much longer than the Theban one, so accepting battle there would have led to a Spartan outflanking manoeuvre. The Thebans also attacked in a way never seen before by the Spartans, their elite left advancing at double speed while their weak right retreated without fighting. The Spartans had never fought against an enemy in this oblique formation and had always been victorious thanks to the decisive power of their elite right wing. It was a brilliant victory for Epaminondas, with 400 of the 700 Spartiates perishing on the battlefield. Sparta was in no position to replace such severe losses. Since the number of Spartiate hoplites had always been quite small, the Spartans had traditionally employed their Peloponnesian allies to field substantial armies and had always tried to preserve as much as possible the lives of their ruling elite. With the death of such a large number of Spartiates, it became clear that the power of Sparta was coming to an end. The few surviving Spartiates would never have been able to generate a sufficient number of male heirs to continue their dominance over the Peloponnese. The traditional allies of Sparta were now considering the possibility of abandoning their 'masters', who were too few to be really dangerous. In 370 BC, after subjugating Orchomenus, the last

Boeotian city that was still an ally of Sparta, the Thebans launched their first invasion of the Peloponnese.

Epaminondas, by now the greatest military leader in Greece, knew full well that thanks to his innovations the Theban army was superior to that of Sparta, and wanted to use this superiority to make Thebes the leading power of mainland Greece as soon as possible. Mantinea, Tegea and most of the Arcadian *poleis* switched sides and abandoned the Peloponnesian League, becoming allies of Thebes and helping Epaminondas in his invasion of the Peloponnese. For the first time in its history, the city of Sparta was menaced by an enemy from outside the Peloponnese. The anti-Spartan alliance, including the Boeotian League, was able to assemble a total of 50,000 soldiers in Arcadia, and in 370 BC these marched south and started the invasion of Lakonia. The decimated Spartan army was in no condition to fight a major battle, and thus all Spartan soldiers remained in their city, ready to defend it againt a Theban siege. The anti-Spartan allies, however, did not attempt to attack Sparta, but simply ravaged the countryside of Lakonia. The vital port of Gythium was raided, as well as Messenia, and the first Theban invasion of the Peloponnese caused enormous economic losses to Sparta, but it did result in a decisive battle. The majority of the Helots were freed, and thus Messenia became independent again after centuries of Spartan rule. The ancient city of Messene, the old capital of the Messenians, was rebuilt, with strong fortifications to prevent any future Spartan attack against the Helots. Sparta had lost a third of its national territory and most of the manpower that was needed to produce enough food for the population.

In 369 BC the anti-Spartan alliance, which had been enlarged with the inclusion of Argos, again invaded the Peloponnese. Fearing that the Thebans could become even more powerful than the Spartans after victory in the Peloponnese, Athens and Corinth had by now formed a military alliance with the Spartiates. The Spartans and their new allies deployed their forces on the Isthmus of Corinth, with the intention of stopping the invaders before they could again ravage Spartan territory. Epaminondas, however, was easily able to break through the defences on the Isthmus and advance south to join his many Peloponnesian allies. However, this second invasion of the Peloponnese did not have the same success as the previous one: a Theban attack against Corinth came to nothing and the arrival of an expedition sent by Syracuse to support Sparta prevented Epaminondas from securing any further victories. A third invasion of the Peloponnese took place in 367 BC, during which the Argives were able to occupy the Isthmus of Corinth before the Spartans, allowing the Thebans to cross it unopposed. Once again, however, this latest Theban attack did not achieve much. Epaminondas tried to gain the support of the Achaean *poleis*, the last allies of Sparta in the Peloponnese, but his attempts came to nothing. At this point of the long war between Thebes and Sparta,

Wicker round shield and javelins of a light infantryman. (*Photo and copyright by Athenea Prómakhos*)

Greek hoplite marching to the field of battle. (*Photo and copyright by Athenea Prómakhos*)

Spartan hoplite with 'muscle' cuirass; on his Corinthian helmet he is wearing the transverse crest typical of Spartiate officers. (*Photo and copyright by Athenea Prómakhos*)

new peace talks, sponsored by the Persians, took place from 367–365 BC, but these were also unsuccessful because the Thebans had no intention to cede Messenia back to Sparta. The Persians then supported Sparta by sending large funds and raising a force of 2,000 mercenaries, so worried were the Achaemenids about the rapid ascendancy of Thebes as a military power. Since their earlier invasions, the Persians had always tried to maintain a balance of power in Greece, since they did not want to see the unification of the *poleis* under a single regional power that could contest Achaemenid supremacy over Asia Minor.

In 365 BC, when hostilities resumed, Corinth and some other minor allies abandoned Sparta. Three years later, Epaminondas launched his final invasion of the Peloponnese with the clear objective of destroying Sparta once and for all. He tried a surprise attack against the city while the Spartan army was away, but this was discovered and failed without any major actions. As a result, the Theban military leader decided that the time had come to fight a decisive pitched battle. This took place at Mantinea in 362 BC and was one of the largest hoplite battles in the history of Greece, involving 33,000 soldiers under the command of Epaminondas against 22,000 troops led by the aging Agesilaus II. As at Leuctra, the Thebans deployed their forces in oblique order and attacked the enemy by surprise. Everything worked perfectly for Epaminondas, whose forces were able to crush the Spartan phalanx after some bitter fighting. However at this point of the clash, when it was clear that the Thebans had achieved another great victory, Epaminondas was killed by a Spartan. Unlike many other military commanders of the time, he had always fought in the first line among his soldiers, which exposed him to the possibility of being mortally wounded. His personal charisma and great knowledge of tactics were fundamental to the success of Thebes, and his unexpected death was a mortal blow for the expansionist ambitions of the Thebans. However, the Spartans suffered serious losses at Mantinea and their time as a leading military power came to an end. At the same time, Thebes abandoned its invasion of the Peloponnese and adopted a new, less aggressive military policy. After many years of terrible internal wars, the Greeks decided to stop all military operations and a new peace treaty was signed by all the *poleis*, with the notable exception of Sparta. Thebes retained prominence over the Boeotian League, but renounced its dream of becoming the leading power of mainland Greece. Sparta relinquished its traditional hegemony over the Peloponnese and Messenia, becoming a secondary actor in the region. Argos and Corinth returned to their previous condition, while Athens benefited from the weakening of Thebes and Sparta. The Athenians were gradually able to restore a great part of the naval and economic influence they had before the Peloponnesian War. The brilliant campaigns of Epaminondas left Greece war-weary and exhausted. Thebes had not been able to exert its dominance over the country and was now obliged to assume a much more defensive military policy.

Greek hoplite from the period of the Peloponnesian War, wearing a nice example of Pilos helmet. (*Photo and copyright by Athenea Prómakhos*)

Thracian peltast equipped with *pelte* shield and javelins. (*Photo and copyright by Athenea Prómakhos*)

Greek hoplite with full heavy infantry panoply, comprising Corinthian helmet and 'muscle' cuirass. (*Photo and copyright by Athenea Prómakhos*)

In 359 BC, just three years after the terrible Battle of Mantineia, Philip II became King of Macedonia, which had long been a semi-barbarous entity located at the northern borders of the Greek world and of little military importance. With the ascendancy of Philip II, everything changed: the new monarch completely reformed the Macedonian army and transformed it into the best military force in the Mediterranean world, abandoning the traditional hoplite tactics and introducing a new panoply for his soldiers. The new Macedonian monarch had lived in Thebes as a royal hostage from 368–365 BC, during which he received an excellent military education from Epaminondas and Pelopidas, learning practically everything of the new hoplite battle tactics. Upon completing the first phase of his reforms, Philip understood that his new military superiority could enable him to transform Macedonia into the 'superpower' of the Greek world. The southern *poleis* were tired of war, lacked manpower and were politically divided. Compared to the single Greek cities, Macedonia was a giant that could gradually absorb all of them. The first target of Philip's expansionist policy towards Greece was Thessaly, which had been recently unified as the Thessalian League by Jason of Pherae in the years up to 370 BC. After Jason's death, however, Thessaly was ravaged by bloody civil wars that saw the participation of Macedonia and Thebes. In 358 BC Philip launched an invasion of Thessaly, in order to have a new government favourable to him in that country. The following year Philip attacked Amphipolis, a strategic Greek city which had previously been an important colony of Athens. The Athenians decided to help Amphipolis against Macedonia, with the objective of reconquering the former colony, but Athens was also fighting on other fronts against a series of rebellions by some of its ex-allies and thus could not send significant reinforcements to Amphipolis. Philip finally conquered Amphipolis, then continued his expansion towards Greece, forming an alliance with the Chalkidian League of northern Greece, obtaining in exchange the city of Potidea, at that time controlled by Athens. He also besieged and conquered the *polis* of Pydna, establishing a strong Macedonian presence in northern Greece. During 354–352 BC Philip intervened again in Thessaly and won a great victory at the Battle of Crocus Field, fought against an alliance comprising Athens and Phocis.

In the years 356–346 BC most of the Greek cities were involved in a new conflict, commonly known as the Third Sacred War because it was caused by the refusal of Phocis to pay a fine imposed by the Temple of Apollo at Delphi, the most important religious institution of Greece. The conflict was mostly fought between Phocis and Thebes, since at that time the latter city controlled the decisions taken by the Temple of Apollo at Delphi and used them for political gain. Phocis was supported by Athens and Sparta, while Thebes could count on the military help of Locris and Macedonia. Philip intervened in the Third Sacred War only to establish a firm Macedonian hegemony over Thessaly, which was full of precious natural resources and linked Macedonia to central Greece. The Thessalian cavalry was of excellent quality and could count on the support of large light infantry contingents. Philip wanted to absorb the Thessalians in his army and expand his domains over the fertile plains of Thessaly. The region contained only a few cities and was, in many ways, more similar to the Kingdom of Macedonia than to the *poleis* of central and southern Greece. Philip occupied most of Thessaly with his army, but was defeated in battle by a substantial military force sent to the region by Phocis. After this temporary setback, the Macedonians reorganized and invaded Thessaly again during the following year. This new campaign ended with their great victory at the Battle of Crocus Field. After this clash, Philip II was appointed archon of Thessaly and became absolute ruler of that region, which was effectively transformed into a vassal state of Macedonia.

Philip attacked his former allies of the Chalkidian League in 349 BC and defeated them after a brilliant campaign. All the cities of the League accepted the Macedonian king as their overlord, except Olynthos, the most important of the Chalkidian *poleis*, which continued to resist. The Macedonians defeated the Olynthians in two pitched battles and then besieged their city. Olynthos was soon taken and razed by Philip, who annexed the whole territory of the Chalkidian League to his realm. Athens was unable to send substantial reinforcements to help Olynthos, because during the same period a coalition of anti-Athenian *poleis* was formed on the island of Euboea. Fearing that the Macedonians could use this event to their advantage, the Athenians sent an army in Euboea to bring the region back into their sphere of influence. The Athenian expedition, however, was a costly failure, so the Euboean cities became allies of Philip II. In 346 BC, since neither Thebes nor Phocis had been able to prevail, the Third Sacred War finally came to an end and Macedonia signed a peace treaty with Athens. The only real victor of the conflict had been Philip, who had used it to conquer most of northern Greece and the vital territory of Thessaly. The terms of the new peace treaty were particularly favourable for Macedonia, since they formally recognized Philip's realm as the most important political actor of the Greek world. In less than 15 years, the new Macedonian monarch had transformed his kingdom from a 'land of barbarians' into a superior military power. After these events, it became clear that the future of Greece would be decided by a clash between Macedonia and Athens.

The Athenians, having not forgotten the fall of Amphipolis, decided to fight against the Macedonian oppressor with all the resources at their disposal. Instigated by the famous orator Demosthenes and his vigorous 'Philippics', the Athenian government tried to form a network of anti-Macedonian military alliances. During the following years, from 340–339 BC, as part of his decisive campaign for the conquest of Greece, Philip besieged two important *poleis* located in the Dardanelles and Hellespont:

Greek hoplite with complete heavy infantry equipment, comprising Corinthian helmet and composite linothorax. (*Photo and copyright by Athenea Prómakhos*)

Greek hoplite from the period of the Peloponnesian War, wearing Chalcidian helmet but no greaves. (*Photo and copyright by Athenea Prómakhos*)

Greek hoplite with Corinthian helmet and linothorax reinforced with bronze scales on the waist. (*Photo and copyright by Athenea Prómakhos*)

Perinthos and Byzantion. The Athenians sent a substantial naval force to support Byzantion, and hostilities recommenced between Philip and Athens. At that time Macedonia did not have a fleet, so the Athenian naval forces were free to help Byzantion. Finally, unable to achieve any significant success, the Macedonians abandoned the sieges of Perinthos and Byzantion in order to move directly against Athens. Philip had decided to organize a final and decisive invasion of Greece, with the clear intention of becoming the supreme commander of the whole Greek world. Fearing Philip's aggressive intent, the Thebans, who had never been his enemies until that moment, decided to side with Athens to save the freedom of the Greeks. The Theban army was still considered the best in mainland Greece and thus, if supported by Athens and other allies, it could have been able to stop the Macedonians. The decisive clash was fought at Chaeronea in 338 BC, where 32,000 Macedonian soldiers commanded by Philip II and his young son Alexander, the future Alexander the Great, faced 35,000 Greeks, comprising mostly Thebans and Athenians, supported by Corinthians and other minor allied contingents. The Greeks fought with enormous courage, but were utterly defeated. Alexander's role in the battle was important in securing victory for his father, but in reality the Greeks were defeated by the superiority of the new Macedonian phalanx. The Thebans resisted as long as they could, but their Sacred Band was completely annihilated: none of the 300 elite hoplites survived, including the unit's commander.

After the Battle of Chaeronea, Philip II treated the Thebans very harshly and practically destroyed their military potential, but the Athenians were spared because the Macedonian monarch needed their fleet in view of his planned campaign against the Persian Empire. All the Greek cities were obliged to accept Macedonian suzerainty, while the most important ones had to admit a Macedonian garrison inside their walls. The Spartans, who had not taken part in the war, initially did not accept Philip's requests, but were in no condition to fight alone against the Macedonians, who ravaged their territories and forced them to accept Macedonia as the ruling power of Greece. In 337 BC Philip II organized the League of Corinth, a confederation of states comprising most of the Greek cities, apart from Sparta, and guided by Macedonia. The Greeks had lost their freedom after centuries: now their soldiers were obliged to fight as allies of the Macedonians and no longer as citizens-soldiers. Under the guidance of Philip's son, Alexander the Great, they would conquer the whole Persian Empire within a few years. Classical Greece had come to an end, and with the rise of Hellenism a new phase of Greek history began.

Chapter 7

Troop Types and Organization of the Greek Armies

Hoplites

The hoplite was the basic soldier of the Greek armies during the Classical Age and remained the best fighter of Antiquity until the ascendancy of the Hellenistic phalangist introduced by Philip II of Macedonia and Alexander the Great. The hoplite was a heavy infantryman and, more importantly, a citizen who had enough economic resources to buy and maintain in perfect efficiency his full panoply of weapons and armour. The latter was designed for close combat and changed little during the period taken into account, having as its most important component the famous round shield, or *hoplon*. Generally speaking, the heavy infantry contingents of the hoplites were organized into regiments, or *taxeis*; these were in turn divided into companies, or *lochoi*. The number of soldiers making up a single *taxis* varied for each city, but usually a regiment comprised 1,000 soldiers from ten *lochoi*; each *lochos*, in fact, generally comprised 100 hoplites. It should be remembered, however, that despite having a quite rigid organization, the citizen-soldiers of the various *poleis* were part-time fighters and not professional warriors: after spending a certain period of his young life (generally one or two years) learning how to use weapons and performing basic unit drill, each citizen-soldier was to be recalled on active service only in time of war. While on service, the hoplites were paid by the state; the latter, however, did not provide or replace any element of the panoply. The officers commanding *lochoi* were little more professional than their men and generally served only during hostilities. The superior commanders of the regiments, however, were professional soldiers with great experience. In most of the cities, both the junior and senior officers were elected by the men under their command or by political assemblies. As time progressed, various *poleis* felt a certain need for professionalism and started to hire professional mercenary officers, who acted as drillmasters and thanks to their experience were generally able to improve the quality of the units assigned to them. From the time of the Peloponnesian War onwards, it became increasingly difficult for the various Greek cities to assemble large numbers of citizen-soldiers, most of whom had started to consider their temporary employment as soldiers as a sort of punishment. The original spirit that had determined the appearance of the hoplite, which linked military duties to political representation, was gradually disappearing. In addition, the new 'total warfare' experienced by Athens

Greek hoplite wearing his Corinthian helmet in the typical position that was used when not fighting. (*Photo and copyright by Athenea Prómakhos*)

Greek hoplite equipped with archaic panoply; note the double decorative crest on his helmet. (*Photo and copyright by Athenea Prómakhos*)

Nice example of bronze 'muscle' cuirass. (*Photo and copyright by Athenea Prómakhos*)

and Sparta during the Peloponnesian War required professional full-time soldiers who could fight in every season of the year and train regularly. As a result, most of the Greek *poleis* started to hire substantial numbers of mercenary hoplites to replace their part-time fighters, who were thus able to dedicate their entire lives to their normal activities, such as commerce. Generally speaking, mercenary hoplites came from the poorest areas of Greece, such as Achaea or Arcadia: these regions had very little by way of natural resources and their terrain was not particularly suitable for agriculture, being covered with hills or mountains. As a result, enlisting as a mercenary was the only chance of earning a living for most of the young males from these regions. Sparta was the only exception to this general rule: the Spartiate citizens did not have a civilian job and were all professional full-time soldiers who trained almost every day from their childhood. They were always ready to be mobilized and their only occupation was war. As time progressed, probably after the Persian Wars, the internal organization of the *lochoi* became more complex, with each company divided into two *pentekostyes* of fifty men each, which were in turn divided into two *enomotia* of twenty-five men each. Each of the latter comprised the following soldiers: twenty-three hoplites, a commander or 'front-rank' officer (the *enomotarch*) and a 'rear-rank' officer (the *ouragos*). The *ouragos* had to maintain order in the ranks and usually killed any hoplites who panicked or abandoned their position in the phalanx. In battle, each of the two *enomotia* was deployed into three files with eight men each, including the *ouragos*. The *enomotarch*, instead, advanced alone at the head of his soldiers. In this organization, each *lochos* was deployed in twelve parallel files with eight men each. The commander of a *lochos* was known as the *lochagos*, while the commander of a *taxis* was a *taxiarch*. Later, with the introduction of *pentekostyes*, the *lochagos* also started to command one of the latter while the other was commanded by a new officer called the *pentekonter*.

Mounted and naval hoplites

Those citizens who were too rich to serve as hoplites and had sufficient economic resources to maintain a horse served as cavalrymen in the army of their city. Since these individuals were generally very few in each city, numbering between 100 and 200, the cavalry contingents of the Greek *poleis* were usually quite small. It could happen, however, that these rich citizens might decide to serve the same as hoplites like the rest of their comrades, in which case they would use their horses only to travel long distances and not employ them during battles. As a result, these richer hoplites acted as a sort of mounted infantry and had greater mobility than the normal hoplites: they could move much more rapidly and could be easily deployed where needed during a battle. This made them elite soldiers, moving as cavalry but fighting as infantry. The 300 royal guardsmen of Leonidas who fought the Persians at the pass of Thermopylae probably belonged to this little-known category of mounted hoplites. They had the same personal equipment of the standard hoplites but did not have proper cavalry training. In contemporary ancient Rome, around 500 BC, the whole cavalry was composed of mounted hoplites, who dismounted to fight; in Greece the situation was different, because as we will see some 'proper' cavalry, fighting on horseback, always existed. We should bear in mind, however, that a certain number of hoplites frequently travelled by horse to reach the battlefield. The poorest citizens of a *poleis* fought as light infantrymen or served as rowers in their city's fleet. These fleets also needed naval infantrymen with heavy equipment who could fight in battles at sea. These did not come from separate bodies of naval infantry, but were the same hoplites who made up the land forces. Despite this, as time progressed, the soldiers called to serve as naval hoplites started to have some peculiarities: for example, when serving on board a warship, a hoplite generally left behind his heavy bronze cuirass and replaced it with a linen one, or even fought without a cuirass. In some cities, such as Athens, when serving in the navy the hoplites also painted specific symbols on their shields, for example elements traditionally linked to Neptune in Greek religion.

Religious sacrifice/ceremony taking place before a hoplite battle. (*Photo and copyright by Athenea Prómakhos*)

Greek hoplites on the field of battle. (*Photo and copyright by Athenea Prómakhos*)

Epilektoi

After the Peloponnesian War, most Greek cities started to form some permanent military units formed of professional soldiers. These chosen fighters, who remained on active service during times of peace, were commonly known as *Epilektoi* (picked soldiers). They were usually chosen from the wealthiest and fittest of the younger citizens, and thus freed from all their public duties. They could therefore train on a regular basis and perform military duties every day, becoming professional soldiers paid and maintained at public expense by their state. Generally speaking, it seems that the basic idea behind the introduction of the *Epilektoi* was that of having a small community of 'Spartiates' in each city. The principal model followed in the various *poleis* was that of the 300 Spartiates who made up the Royal Guard of the Spartan monarchs. In most of the cities, the *Epilektoi* numbered no more than 300 or 400. This was the case of the most famous of all the elite units, the Sacred Band of Thebes, which comprised 300 skilled fighters (see below for more details on this corps). In some cities the *Epilektoi* could be more numerous, such as in Argos where there were 1,000 in total. In case of full-scale war, the *Epilektoi* of each city would form the nucleus of professional soldiers around which the rest of the army was to be assembled, the latter being made up of citizen-hoplites or mercenaries. The contingents of picked soldiers became extremely popular during the fifth century BC, when most of the Greek citizens started to consider military service as a negative compulsory activity. The various cities reacted to this problem by organizing small *Epilektoi* units and recruiting large numbers of mercenaries. With the ascendancy of the professional soldiers, be they *Epilektoi* or mercenaries, the heavy standard hoplite equipment was once again complete. Cuirasses and greaves, the use of which had been largely abandoned inside the mass armies that fought in the Peloponnesian War, started to be employed again on a regular basis. Each state spent large sums of money to provide the best panoply to its few professional soldiers, while the mercenaries had to buy their own equipment with the economic resources they had. The re-adoption of cuirasses and greaves was also partly due to the military reforms of Philip II, who gave a light cuirass to all his new phalangists.

Peltasts

Until the end of the Persian Wars, Greek armies were mostly made up of hoplite heavy infantry supported by small contingents of auxiliary troops (cavalry, light infantry archers and slingers). A certain number of the poorest citizens served as javelineers, but the latter were rarely used in battle and were of little use against the close tactical formations of the hoplites. During the Persian Wars, however, the Greeks, for the first time, had to face large numbers of enemy light infantrymen with peculiar equipment: these were the Persian 'Takabara', Iranian or Anatolian skirmishers who carried a crescent-shaped wickerwork shield and a light axe. The Takabara were easily defeated by the hoplites when fighting in close combat, but proved to be superior to their Greek opponents during skirmishing and reconnaissance operations. Thanks to their light equipment, they were much more mobile than a Greek heavy infantryman. After the Persian defeat, the Greeks – in particular the Athenians – started to extend their sphere of political influence over some Balkan regions that had been previously dominated by the Achaemenids. This was the case with Thrace, with which the Greeks had experienced little contact before the Persian Wars. Since this region was extremely rich in natural resources, Greek military expeditions in Thrace became increasingly frequent around the middle of the fifth century BC. In Thrace the Greek hoplites met another kind of enemy soldier who had light infantry equipment and fought very similarly to the Persian Takabara: the peltast. Each Thracian tribal warrior was a peltast, the term deriving from the *pelte* shield carried by all Thracian foot soldiers. Like that of the Takabara, this was a crescent-shaped wicker shield, very light and perfectly suited for a light infantry use. Most of the territory of Thrace (present-day Bulgaria) was covered by mountains and hills, where on such terrain it was impossible to deploy troops in mass close formations like that of the Greek phalanx. The Thracian warriors were used to fight as skirmishers, their wars being mostly inter-tribal conflicts with the raiding of bordering villages and cattle rustling. They wore no armour and were armed in most cases with only light javelins, which were perfect for their hit-and-run guerrilla tactics and could be used to kill the enemy from a distance, for example during the frequent ambushes that were employed. Initially the Greek hoplites had great difficulties in fighting against the Thracians, moving too slowly to respond effectively to their opponents' rapid attacks. As a result, some Greek commanders started to introduce a new category of 'lighter' hoplites known as *Ekdromoi*. This measure, however, proved incapable of facing such a rapid enemy as the Thracians, and thus the Greeks had to introduce peltasts in their own armies. To begin with this was done by simply recruiting large numbers of Thracian mercenaries, which were always available, but as time progressed the Greek cities started to train and equip some of their citizen-soldiers as peltasts rather than hoplites. Basically, in the Greek military system, a peltast was a 'medium' infantryman: they did not have helmet or armour, but did carry a shield, unlike the traditional light infantry of the javelineers and slingers. The *pelte* was crescent-shaped in order to ease the throwing of javelins. Each peltast could throw a javelin from the convex top of the shield while protecting his torso behind the concave section. Instead of a helmet, the Thracian peltasts wore a cap made of fox-skin, perfectly suited to the cold temperatures of the Thracian winters

Line of Greek hoplites deployed on the battlefield. (*Photo and copyright by Athenea Prómakhos*)

Greek hoplites standing on the battlefield in close formation. (*Photo and copyright by Athenea Prómakhos*)

Greek officer with Corinthian helmet and linothorax. (*Photo and copyright by Athenea Prómakhos*)

thanks to the presence of a pair of earflaps. A square cloak and a long tunic, both very thick, were also worn. The traditional Thracian dress was completed by a pair of fur-lined fawn-skin boots, which were perfect to run on terrain covered with snow. The fur lining fell in three folds, which was distinctively Thracian. The new Greek peltasts did not have the same traditional dress as the original Thracian ones, but did use the same basic equipment with *pelte* shield and light javelins. They never became as important as the hoplites, but did obtain some significant victories against the heavy infantry during the Peloponnesian War.

Ekdromoi

The *Ekdromoi* were the first response of the Greek commanders to the new challenge represented by the Thracian peltasts. Basically, the *Ekdromoi* were the youngest and fittest of the hoplites of a phalanx, who did not wear armour or greaves and were expected to run out of the line in order to catch up with the Thracian peltasts before they could flee the battlefield after having thrown their javelins. The term *Ekdromoi* (singular *Ekdromos*) simply means 'out-runners'. As stated above, the creation of this new category of 'light hoplites' was not enough to overcome the Thracians, and thus the Greeks had to introduce peltasts into their own armies. It is important to underline, however, that the *Ekdromoi* had a great influence over the development of the basic hoplite panoply. Over time, it became clear that the lighter combination of only helmet and shield employed by the *Ekdromoi* gave a reasonable amount of protection while at the same time considerably increasing mobility. As a result, most of the Greek hoplites started to abandon the regular use of cuirasses and greaves, and by the beginning of the Peloponnesian War, virtually all the Greek hoplites were equipped as *Ekdromoi* rather than as their ancestors had fought in the Persian Wars. Armour and greaves were partially reintroduced only during the latter years of the period taken into account in this book, due to the ascendancy of professional hoplites (*Epilektoi*) and to the emergence of the Macedonian phalangists, who wore light cuirasses.

Psiloi

From 500 BC most of the Greek cities deployed armies almost entirely made up of hoplites, but there were some small contingents of light infantrymen with auxiliary duties. These comprised the poorest citizens of each *polis* who could not afford the complete hoplite panoply. In the case of naval operations, these individuals would serve as rowers for the fleet, but during land operations, most of the poorest individuals went to the field of battle with their ordinary clothes and no armour. They were equipped with rudimentary weapons – mostly javelins and stones – and had no specific training to speak of. These light infantrymen with no particular specialization were commonly known as *Psiloi* and had a distinctly secondary role during battles. Due to their lack

Greek hoplites exulting at the end of a battle. (*Photo and copyright by Athenea Prómakhos*)

Thessalian light infantryman with the peculiar sun hat and cloak of his region; he is equipped with *pelte* shield and javelins. (*Photo and copyright by Athenea Prómakhos*)

Duel between two Thessalian light infantrymen, fighting with javelins. (*Photo and copyright by Athenea Prómakhos*)

of training and minimal equipment, they did not represent a serious menace to the heavy-armoured hoplite. When peltasts appeared in the Greek armies, the importance of the *Psiloi* decreased markedly, the peltasts proving superior to all the other light infantrymen thanks to their use of the *pelte* shield. The *Psiloi* regained some importance during the Peloponnesian War, when Athens was obliged by circumstances to employ all its available citizens, with those who were too old or too young to serve in the army temporarily enlisted to fight as *Psiloi*. They could be useful during siege operations – for example to defend the walls of their city – or as explorers/skirmishers. Since they wore no helmet and did not have armour or shield, the *Psiloi* could move quite rapidly on every kind of terrain, especially on broken ground. In Aetolia, a region of Greece where most of the territory was covered by mountains or hills and the population lived in many small villages, the *Psiloi* represented the majority of the local fighters, with hoplites practically absent. The Aetolian *Psiloi*, armed only with javelins and stones, were particularly effective during ambushes and skirmishes, proving able to repulse

Greek hoplites on the field of battle. (*Photo and copyright by Athenea Prómakhos*)

Greek hoplites resting before a battle. (*Photo and copyright by Athenea Prómakhos*)

several enemy invasions of their territory in the period under discussion. Each *Psilos* usually wore a shaggy felt hat and a tunic of coarse cloth, that being the basic dress of the Greek peasant or shepherd. Most of the *Psiloi* fought barefoot and did not have any kind of body protection, although sometimes they could carry a makeshift shield consisting of an animal pelt laid along the left arm, secured in place by knotting a pair of the paws around the neck. In addition to Aetolia, Thessaly also had some excellent light infantry *Psiloi*. Neither of these regions had many proper cities, nor many hoplites. Most of the Thessalian foot troops were equipped as javelineers, but unlike the other Greek *Psiloi* these usually carried a small round shield.

Hamippoi

The *Hamippoi* were a specialized sub-category of the *Psiloi*, created in Sicily by Gelon of Syracuse and later exported to mainland Greece before the Peloponnesian War. The Syracusan army contained a large number of excellent cavalrymen, which, differently from what happened in Greece, were more important than the hoplites and were an elite force. During the period 490–480 BC, when Gelon was tyrant of Syracuse, the

Greek hoplite officer in full archaic panoply. (*Photo and copyright by Athenea Prómakhos*)

Greeks of Sicily fought a fierce war against the Carthaginians who were expanding in the island from their original bases on the western coast. During this conflict, in order to support his numerous horsemen in the clashes against the Carthaginian heavy cavalry, Gelon created a new category of light infantrymen, initially known as *Hippodromoi Psiloi*, or '*Psiloi* who run alongside with the cavalry'. These, who would later become simply known as *Hamippoi*, were *Psiloi* light infantrymen having specific equipment and training, which derived from their peculiar tactical function: they had to go into battle running behind the horse of a cavalryman, holding on to the tail or mane of the horse. In battle they had to slip underneath the horses of the enemy cavalrymen and rip open their bellies, for which they were equipped with a short dagger, used to strike the enemy horses, and trained to run for long distances with the cavalry. Like all the *Psiloi* they had no body armour and simply wore a felt hat. In theory, each cavalryman was supported by one *Hamippos*, but this rarely happened. The *Sciritae*, light infantrymen of the Spartan army, were converted into *Hamippoi* (see below).

Slingers

Slingers represent an important part of the *Psiloi*. They were equipped with simple self-made slings, which could be quite effective against hoplites if used from a medium distance. In addition to the *Psiloi* slingers, who were not professional soldiers and thus did not have specific training with their weapon, Greek armies of the Classical period included contingents of professional mercenary slingers from the island of Rhodes. During Antiquity, the major islands of the Mediterranean produced and exported large numbers of mercenaries with very particular light infantry specializations: archers from Crete and slingers from the Balearic Islands and Rhodes. This was mostly due to the scarce natural resources existing on these islands, which were not sufficient to feed a large population. As a result, many of the young males from these poor communities had no choice but to serve abroad as mercenaries. In Rhodes, the sling was virtually a national weapon, used by young and adult males practically every day to hunt. Trained since childhood, the Rhodian slingers were able to hit very small targets from long distances with deadly precision. They were also able to produce a rain of projectiles if employed in substantial numbers, but this happened quite rarely on Greek battlefields. Rhodian slingers were acquired as mercenaries by several *poleis* because of their superior skills compared to those of the ordinary slingers from mainland Greece. Their slings were made of cloth or sinew, and launched projectiles ranging from half-pound shaped slugs to rocks found on the battlefield. Longer and shorter versions of the basic sling also existed, for use from different distances.

Archers

Since the Mycenean period, bows were largely employed in Greece as light infantry weapons, as well as for hunting. With the introduction of the hoplite heavy infantry, however, archers started to be of very little military use since their arrows were not a serious menace for the large shields of the hoplites. However, most of the Greek armies continued to have a certain number of archers during the period under examination. These light soldiers wore no armour and could belong to two different categories, like the slingers: they could be poor citizens from the lower social classes of their *polis* or professional mercenaries from Crete. The archers belonging to the first category were not so different from the *Psiloi*, but had self-made wooden bows and some experience as hunters. They were not particularly effective and were no match for the superior Persian archers. The Cretan mercenaries, on the other hand, were professional fighters who underwent specific training as archers from childhood and used a superior model of bow. During the Classical period, the island of Crete was mostly covered with dense forests where hunters could find large quantities of boars and deer. Since there were

Detail of a hoplite in close combat formation, equipped with Chalcidian helmet. (*Photo and copyright by Athenea Prómakhos*)

Greek hoplites fighting in the front line with their spears. (*Photo and copyright by Athenea Prómakhos*)

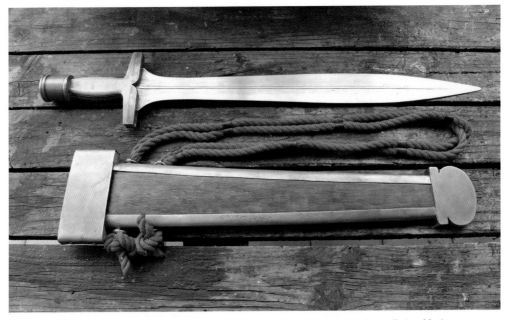

Nice example of *xiphos* short sword. (*Photo and copyright by Athenea Prómakhos*)

no other significant natural resources, all the young and adult males of Crete had to learn how to hunt with their bows from the very early years of their life. Cretan archers used a deadly model of bow created from two pieces of wood rather than a single one, which enabled them to shoot with greater power and accuracy than their equivalents from mainland Greece. In addition, thanks to their intensive training, they were able to fire an impressive number of arrows in a very short time. Cretan archers usually wore a head-band to absorb sweat and leather boots that were perfect to walk on broken terrain. They also carried small round shields made of bronze, which were worn attached to the left arm while firing an arrow. These little shields, which were not employed by the archers from mainland Greece, gave the Cretan ones a certain tactical superiority since they could defend themselves from enemy arrows when fighting in open terrain. The basic equipment of a Cretan archer was completed by a quiver made of leather and a little bag of the same material containing arrowheads and bowstrings that was worn around the neck. Thanks to their quality, similarly to the Rhodian slingers, the Cretan archers were sought in every corner of the Mediterranean and were paid very well for their military services.

Cavalry

Around 500 BC, cavalry was very much a secondary element of Greek warfare, since the armies of the various *poleis* generally included very few horsemen, usually just a few hundred. This was largely due to two factors: most of Greece was covered by mountains or hills and thus was not suitable for breeding large numbers of good quality horses, and only the richest citizens of each *polis* could sustain the expense of maintaining a war horse for a long time. As we have seen, this meant that frequently those few rich citizens who could afford horses would actually decide to fight as hoplites and employ their horses only to travel long distances, acting as mounted hoplites. Two areas of Greece were an exception to this general rule: Thessaly and Boeotia, whose territory consisted of flat plains with excellent pastures for horses. As a result, these were the only regions of Greece where cavalry was dominant from a military point of view. However, this situation eventually changed when the Boeotian *poleis* became increasingly important and more populated, which led to the adoption of the urban hoplite military system and a gradual decrease in importance of Boeotian cavalry. This did not happen in Thessaly, where the few cities remained quite isolated and did not acquire great political importance. The Thessalians continued to fight as cavalrymen for all the Classical period, never adopting the hoplite military system on a large scale. The Thessalian terrain was perfect for rearing cattle and growing grain, enabling the local aristocrats to become rich, thanks to the export of these important products. The

Bronze bell cuirass, heavily decorated. (*Photo and copyright by Athenea Prómakhos*)

Thessalians, be they aristocrats or commoners, were used to riding from their early childhood, as well as to fighting as deadly light cavalrymen armed with javelins. They did not wear armour, helmet or shield; mobility and speed were the key factors of their success. The Thessalian horsemen were excellent skirmishers who loved to use hit-and-run tactics and to fight from a distance with their throwing weapons. In order to ride more comfortably, a distinctive Thessalian 'riding dress' was developed during the Classical period, which included the famous wide-brimmed sun-hat known as the *petasos*, which protected its wearer from the heat and dust during the summer months. A metal version of the *petasos* eventually became popular, a helmet with the same shape as the original sun-hat. Thessalian cavalrymen also wore a long and enveloping cloak, which was used in combination with a tunic during winter or worn on the naked body during summer. Thin cavalry boots, of the same kind employed by all the other Greek horsemen, could also be worn, but frequently the Thessalians rode barefoot. The Thessalian 'riding dress' became so popular that all the cavalrymen of Greece, even those from Athens, adopted it to look similar to the skilled horsemen of Thessaly. The Thessalian cavalry frequently served outside their region as mercenaries or allies

Bronze greaves. (*Photo and copyright by Athenea Prómakhos*)

Composite cuirass consisting of a linothorax reinforced with a band of bronze scales. Two lines of *pteruges* are clearly visible in the lower part. (*Photo and copyright by Athenea Prómakhos*)

of the various Greek military leagues. Having a contingent of Thessalian cavalrymen frequently proved a decisive factor in winning a battle. In addition to javelins, Thessalian horsemen also employed a long cavalry lance known as the *kamax*, which was designed to strike enemy infantrymen while charging and enabled the Thessalians to act as 'shock' cavalry if needed. Slashing swords could also be carried, especially by the richest individuals. From a political point of view, Thessaly was traditionally divided into four tetrarchies, or districts, which formed a loose confederation known as the Thessalian League that was guided by a *tagos*, or supreme leader. Each tetrarchy was divided into a certain number of *kleroi* (lots), each of which provided forty cavalrymen and eighty infantrymen to the Thessalian League for military service. Since Thessaly had a total of 150 *kleroi*, the Thessalian League could deploy a total of 12,000 infantry and 6,000 cavalry. The number of horsemen was impressive, being greatly superior to the number of cavalry that could be assembled by all the cities of Greece. The Thessalian infantry was a mix of light troops, including peltasts, *Psiloi* and *Ekdromoi*. The Thessalian military organization was reformed only at a very late date by Jason of Pherae, who tried to modernize his forces after becoming *tagos* in 374 BC. Jason abolished the *kleroi* and established cities as the territorial unit from which the military contingents had to be levied. He also introduced a new rhomboid formation for his excellent cavalry, which proved unstoppable during attacks and later evolved into the famous wedge formation employed with enormous success by Philip II and Alexander the Great.

The Athenian Army

The Athenian army was a perfect example of how a Greek army of the Classical Age could be organized. Each of the ten traditional Athenian tribes provided a *taxis*, or regiment, with 1,000 hoplites, and each *taxis* comprised ten *lochoi*, or companies. Each of the ten tribes was also to provide a *phyle*, or squadron, of cavalry, with 100 horsemen. As a result, the standard army on campaign comprised 10,000 hoplites and 1,000 cavalrymen. Before 442 BC, the Athenian cavalry comprised just 300 horsemen and had very little military importance; during that year, however, it was completely reformed and increased to 1,000 soldiers, mostly young and rich individuals. The ten *phyle* were generally assembled into two groups of five, known as *hipparchies*, each of which was deployed on one of the phalanx's flanks to protect the hoplites from attacks by the enemy cavalry and light infantry. Each cavalry squadron could be divided into two sub-units of fifty men, commanded by a specific officer. In addition, the 100 soldiers of a *phyle* were divided into groups of ten men, commanded by an inferior officer known as a *dekadarchos*. Unlike the infantry, the Athenian cavalry was deployed in files with ten men in each, which would justify the presence of the *dekadarchos* as front-line commander. Apparently, like the infantry, there was also a rear-rank officer to prevent desertions from the back of the formation.

Each Athenian citizen had to undergo two years of military training upon reaching the age of 18. This period of compulsory military service was known as the *ephebate*, with each recruit thus commonly known as an *ephebus*. The first year consisted of a basic military training course, which was common for all citizens and was carried out in special barracks built at Piraeus, the port of Athens. During the second year, the training was different for each category of *ephebus*: the richest ones, serving as cavalrymen, learned how to ride and use their specific weapons (javelins and *kamax*), while the majority, serving as hoplites, learned close-combat tactics and manned the frontier forts that protected Attica, and the poorest individuals, serving as light infantrymen, patrolled the countryside of Attica and were thus known as *peripoloi*, or patrollers.

In 442 BC the Athenian mounted troops were further augmented with the creation of a new special corps, the *Hippotoxotai*, or horse archers. The 200 *Hippotoxotai* were divided into two sub-units of 100 men, each of which was attached to one of the *hipparchies*. The horse archers were elite light cavalrymen, mostly acting as skirmishers and scouts/couriers. From a tactical point of view, the *Hippotoxotai* were more mounted archers than horse archers: they did not fire arrows from horseback, as did the Persian light cavalry, but simply used their horses to travel long distances. In practice, the *Hippotoxotai* were very similar to the mounted hoplites described above, a highly mobile force of chosen light infantry. In 395 BC, probably as part of Iphicrates' early military reforms, the *Hippotoxotai* were abolished. In that same year, to substitute the latter in their functions, the Athenian government created a new cavalry unit whose members became known as *Prodromoi*, meaning 'runners-ahead'; in fact the *Prodromoi* were light cavalrymen acting as skirmishers and scouts/couriers. The 200 *Hippotoxotai* had been originally recruited from the lower social classes of Athens, as a distinct corps from the 1,000 *hippeis* (regular cavalry). The *Prodromoi*, however, were not formed by recruiting new soldiers but by simply detaching some of the ordinary horsemen from their units. Each of the Athenian cavalry squadrons selected five of its best members to act as *Prodromoi*. As a result, in total, the Athenian army comprised just fifty such elite scouts. These were assembled into two groups (one for each of the *hipparchies*) with twenty-five soldiers each. The *Prodromoi* did not wear cuirasses, unlike the *Hippotoxotai*, and had javelins as their main weapon.

The light troops of the Athenian army also comprised a special force of 'Scythian' archers, which was raised in 490 BC and comprised 300 soldiers. We have very few details about this exotic military unit in Athenian service, but what we do know is that it was made up of foreigners who were slaves in Athens. Considering that the corps was formed shortly after the Battle of Marathon, it is probable that these 'Scythian' archers could have come from the many Persian prisoners captured by the Athenians at Marathon. Other sources, however, state that the original 300 'Scythian' archers were all slaves bought from the Black Sea region by the Athenian government. The Scythians are listed among the allied contingents that fought for the Persians during the campaign of 490 BC, so it could be possible that the 300 who entered Athenian service were effectively prisoners of war. At the same time, it was common practice for the Athenians to buy large amounts of slaves from Thrace and the Black Sea. In any case, the 'Scythian' archers acted as an elite police corps inside the city of Athens. They were equipped as soldiers with the traditional composite bow employed by the Scythians, but mostly performed police duties, their main function being to maintain

Greek hoplite wearing Pilos helmet. (*Photo and copyright by Athenea Prómakhos*)

Greek hoplite with Chalcidian helmet and linothorax. (*Photo and copyright by Athenea Prómakhos*)

Chalcidian, Illyrian and Corinthian helmets (from left to right). (*Photo and copyright by Athenea Prómakhos*)

order during public gatherings and act as watchmen/guards for public buildings. From a legal point of view, they were public slaves and thus the property of the Athenian government. The 300 'Scythian' archers were separated from the other Athenian archers of the army, who performed purely military functions and numbered 1,200. Ancient sources do not contain precise details about the internal organization of the latter, but since their total number was the same as the cavalry – 1,000 *hippeis* plus 200 *Hippotoxotai* – it could be possible that the Athenian archers comprised 100 men from each of the ten tribes plus 200 'chosen' men recruited from the lower social classes, as were the 'horse archers'). As time progressed, the original 300 'Scythian' archers started to be replaced by other public slaves of foreign nationality, who continued to be dressed and equipped as Scythians. Using foreign slaves as policemen was probably the result of a definite choice, since they did not have any link with the political parties of Athens and thus were completely neutral in performing their duties. A citizen or an

Nice example of Corinthian helmet, painted in red. (*Photo and copyright by Athenea Prómakhos*)

A couple of hoplites supported by a Scythian archer; the red shield is of the Boeotian type (different from the round *hoplon*). (*Photo and copyright by Athenea Prómakhos*)

Greek hoplite with Corinthian helmet and linothorax. (*Photo and copyright by Athenea Prómakhos*)

Athenian slave could have been easily influenced by one of the factions that fought for power. We have no idea when the 'Scythian' archers were disbanded, but this probably happened in 395 BC, when the *Hippotoxotai* were also abolished.

At the beginning of the fourth century BC, an innovative general named Iphicrates completely reformed the Athenian army by changing the standard panoply of the hoplites and peltasts. Iphicrates' reforms, which were revolutionary for the time, did not save the Athenian army from its slow decline but did have a fundamental impact on the development of the new Macedonian phalanx introduced by Philip II. As we will see, the new Macedonian phalangist was just an improved version of the lesser-known Iphicratean hoplite. Iphicrates was the first who saw the great potential of the peltasts as a sort of 'medium infantry', which could fight both as light skirmishers and as heavy shock troops according to circumstances. In 391 BC, at the Battle of Lechaeum, Iphicrates was able to defeat a contingent of Spartan hoplites with just a force of peltasts, for the first time in Spartan history. During the previous years, he had already modified the panoply and tactics of the Athenian peltasts: instead of the traditional *pelte* shield, Iphicrates gave his peltasts a large oval wicker shield, while they also wore a helmet for head protection. Offensive weapons now included a short sword and short spear, in addition to the usual javelins. Thanks to the larger shield and new helmet, the Iphicratean peltast could fight in close combat against a hoplite, and the new sword and spear gave him more or less the same offensive capabilities as a heavy infantryman. Compared to a hoplite, however, this new peltast was much more mobile since he wore no armour. In practice, Iphicrates had completed the transition of the peltast from a light infantryman to a medium one. After the positive experience of Lechaeum, the Athenian general also decided to modify the panoply and tactics of the standard hoplite: the large *hoplon* was abandoned in favour of a much smaller and lighter round shield; the metal greaves were discarded and replaced by new comfortable leather boots known as *Iphicratids*, from the name of their creator; new lighter cuirasses made of quilted linen replaced the older models; and the spear, to compensate the lightening of the defensive equipment, was lengthened to 3.6 metres. The new small shield could be strapped to the forearm, thus freeing the left hand to help holding the new longer model of spear. Iphicrates made the panoply of the peltasts heavier and that of the hoplites lighter. Philip II adopted the equipment prescribed by the Athenian general for the new hoplites as the standard panoply of his Macedonian phalangists. Unfortunately the Iphicratean reforms were not adopted in other Greek cities, while even in Athens they never had a universal diffusion. If the reforms had been standardized, the Greeks may well have been able to face the expanding Macedonian Army on equal terms, with much more chance of victory.

The Spartan Army

Originally the Spartiate population had been divided into three tribes, but when hoplite military formations were introduced in Sparta the citizens had already been reorganized on five administrative entities known as *obai*, or villages. Each of these was to provide one *lochos*, or company, of hoplites, with 900 men organized into thirty *triakades* of thirty men each. As a result, Spartan *lochoi* were much stronger than the Athenian ones since they were comparable to regiments rather than companies. In total, the early Spartan army could deploy 4,500 hoplites (900 for each of the five *obai*). By the outbreak of the Persian Wars, this original organization had been abandoned and the number of hoplites had been increased to 5,000, probably due to a general expansion of the Spartan population. Each of the five *lochoi* was now to comprise 1,000 hoplites, the exact equivalent of an Athenian *taxis*, or regiment. The 1,000 soldiers were structured on twenty *pentekostyes* of fifty men each, which replaced the old *triakades*. Due to the high losses suffered during the second half of the fifth century BC, and especially during the long Peloponnesian War, the Spartan army was greatly reduced in numbers and thus had to be completely reorganized. Now it included just 2,560 Spartiate hoplites, more or less half of the soldiers who were deployed in the most crucial phase of the Persian Wars. These were structured on five smaller *lochoi*, with 512 hoplites each. A single *lochos* comprised four *pentekostyes* of a new type, with 128 soldiers each. Each of the *pentekostyes* was in turn divided into four *enomotiai* with thirty-two hoplites each.

After the disastrous defeat of Mantineia the number of Spartiate hoplites was strongly reduced again due to the casualties suffered in battle. The military organization of Sparta was then changed again, and for the first time the Spartiates were obliged to accept the *Perioikoi* in their ranks. Without the inclusion of the latter, Sparta would have not been able to field a sizeable military force. The Spartan army was now divided into six *morai*, or divisions, each numbering 576 hoplites and 100 cavalrymen. A single *mora* comprised four *lochoi* of 144 infantrymen each, with the *lochos* structured on two *pentekostyes* with seventy-two hoplites. Each of the *pentekostyes* comprised two *enomotiai* of thirty-six men. In total, with the inclusion of the *Perioikoi*, the Spartans were now able to deploy 3,456 hoplites in six divisions, which were clearly too few to confront the new enemies of Sparta, and furthermore the quality of the *Perioikoi* could not be compared with that of the former Spartiate hoplites. With the introduction of the *morai*, the previous recruiting system based on the five traditional tribes was completely abandoned. By the time Macedonia started to fight against the Greek cities, the Spartan army numbered just 1,728 hoplites: these were still organized into six *morai*, but each division was now to comprise just two *lochoi* instead of four. Before their admission into the Spartiate ranks, the *Perioikoi* had already fought as hoplites but in separate contingents. These numbered about 5,000 soldiers by the time Sparta was the dominant military power of Greece.

During most of the period taken into account here, each Spartiate hoplite was always accompanied on the field of battle by one or more Helot servants, acting mostly as baggage-carriers but also frequently employed as light infantry *Psiloi*, armed with missile weapons and dressed in caps/clothes made from animal skins. Around 420 BC, in a desperate attempt to increase the number of hoplites in their army, the Spartiates started to free some selected groups of Helots and to equip them as heavy infantrymen. These formed their own independent units and became known as *neodamodeis*, but, unlike the Periokoi, they were never admitted into the *morai* and were recruited only from the Helots of Lakonia, who were more loyal to Sparta than the Messenian ones. The *neodamodeis* were organized on two *lochoi*, but always remained 'half-citizens', having a social status comparable to that of the *Perioikoi* before their admission into the Spartiates' ranks. They did not fight for their former masters with great enthusiasm, their only motivation being that of defending their newly acquired freedom.

Cavalry was never considered an important branch of the army in Sparta, the only notable exception to this rule being represented by Leonidas' 300-strong royal guard of mounted hoplites. In Sparta the most prominent citizens, the only ones who could own horses, all preferred to serve in the infantry as normal hoplites and thus did not form the bulk of the mounted troops as in other Greek states. As a result, the few horsemen of the Spartan army were not aristocrats but Spartiates of modest social origins. These individuals did not have a personal horse nor the economic resources to equip the latter for war, as a result of which the Spartan state required its most prominent citizens to provide their horses for military service and give them to the soldiers assigned to the cavalry. The cavalry recruits were usually chosen because of their weak physical constitution, comprising soldiers who were not strong enough to serve as heavy infantrymen but young enough to fight. Horses were provided by the richest citizens, including the *Perioikoi*, only in time of war, and thus the Spartan cavalry long remained a temporary corps. It was only in 442 BC, to face the dangerous threat represented by Athenian incursions, that the Spartan government decided to create a permanent body of cavalry, with 400 horsemen. The latter were organized into four *lochoi* with 100 soldiers each. When the Spartan army was restructured on six divisions, each of them received a *lochos* of horsemen, and thus the cavalry contingent was augmented from 400 to 600 soldiers. Each cavalry *lochos* was divided into two *oulamoi* of fifty men; each *oulamos* comprised ten *dekas* of ten men and each of the *dekas* was structured on two *pempas* of five men.

The Spartiates generally despised any form of light infantry warfare. According to their own peculiar view of the world, fighting from distance was only fit for cowards:

Greek hoplite attacking with his spear. (*Photo and copyright by Athenea Prómakhos*)

Greek hoplite with Pilos helmet and shield painted with a Sphinx emblem. (*Photo and copyright by Athenea Prómakhos*)

Hoplites deployed in close defensive formation. (*Photo and copyright by Athenea Prómakhos*)

true men had to fight as hoplites, to prove to everyone their value. Until 425 BC the Spartan army did not comprise contingents of archers, which were considered to be of no use during hoplite clashes. After the disaster of Sphacteria, however, the Spartiates understood that a certain amount of archers was needed to face the Athenian light troops on almost equal terms. Since Lakonia and Messenia had no significant archery traditions, the Spartans had to rely on Cretan mercenaries. These accompanied Spartan military contingents during most of the campaigns fought after 425 BC, being organized into small but highly effective contingents of 200–300 archers.

While a Spartiate would have never served as a light infantryman armed with missile weapons, the Spartans could count on the precious military support of a little-known allied community in order to deploy a sizeable and effective light infantry force. These were the *Sciritae*, a small group of people subject to Sparta, whose social status was comparable to that of the *Perioikoi*. They were loyal allies of the Spartiates, but enjoyed a quite high degree of autonomy. The *Sciritae* lived on the northern border of Lakonia in a harsh and mountainous terrain. Their communities inhabited small rural villages and were used to protect the northern borders of the Spartan state from incursions by the warlike Arcadians, whose southern territories were located north of the *Sciritae* settlements. Having no proper urban centres to speak of and living mostly as shepherds or farmers in a mountainous territory, the *Sciritae* were used to fight as light infantry skirmishers from their childhood and had no idea of hoplite warfare. In exchange for Spartan political and military protection, they were required to provide the Spartan army with an elite contingent of 600 light infantrymen organized into a single *lochos*. The *Sciritae* were formidable scouts, and although equipped similarly to the standard *Psiloi* of the time they had far superior combat capabilities than any other light infantry contingent in Classical Greece. If needed, they could also be equipped as hoplites and fight on the side of the Spartiates in case of emergency. They were used to all kinds of physical privation and could travel enormous distances in a very short time. When the Spartan army was reorganized on six divisions and the cavalry increased to 600 men, the *Sciritae* were transformed into *Hamippoi* light infantry, each of whom was assigned to a cavalryman. They largely continued to perform their usual tactical functions, but with a higher degree of coordination with the cavalry. In addition to the *Sciritae*, after the end of the Peloponnesian War the Spartans started to deploy some contingents of mercenary peltasts in order to augment their light infantry forces. These were not of excellent quality, but were necessary to face the light troops deployed by Sparta's enemies. After the Battle of Leuktra, in 371 BC, the *Sciritae* became independent from the Spartiates, who had to rely entirely on their mercenary peltasts in order to have some light infantry.

The Theban Army

Around 395 BC the army of the Boeotian League, comprising also that of Thebes, deployed a total of 11,000 hoplites and 1,100 cavalrymen. These numbers were comparable to those of the Athenian military forces, but it must be remembered that the Boeotian League was a confederation of several *poleis* guided by Thebes and not a single Greek state. Boeotia was divided into eleven territorial districts, four of which belonged to Thebes' direct possessions. Each district elected a supreme military commander, known as a *boeotarch*, and raised 1,100 soldiers, made up of 1,000 hoplites and 100 cavalrymen. Thebes alone could field 4,000 hoplites and 400 horsemen, a military force comparable to that of the Spartiates. The Theban contingent of the army of the Boeotian League also comprised a special unit of 300 *Epilektoi* (chosen soldiers): the *Hieros Lochos*, or Sacred Band, probably the most famous military unit of Classical Greece. The hoplites who made up this unit were all full-time professional soldiers, who formed the permanent garrison of Thebes and were stationed in their city's most important fortress, the Cadmeia. The Sacred Band was probably created around 378 BC by Gorgidas, after Pelopidas expelled the Spartan military garrison that had been installed in the Cadmeia. Pelopidas later became commander of the new

Hoplites deployed in close combat formation; note the use of a leather curtain to protect the lower legs (attached to the bottom part of the shield). (*Photo and copyright by Athenea Prómakhos*)

corps, and it is highly probable that in this early phase the Sacred Band was entirely made up of Theban exiles who had reconquered their city with Athenian military help. As a result, this chosen unit had a strong democratic imprinting from its early beginnings. Essentially, the Sacred Band was formed by the Thebans in order to have an elite corps that could face the professional Spartiate hoplites on almost equal terms, so the elite *lochos* of 300 men was given the best equipment and received the best training. In 338 BC, at the Battle of Chaeronea, the Sacred Band was crushed by the Macedonians and all its members were killed after putting up a heroic resistance.

The Argive Army

Unfortunately we know very little about the Argive army of the Classical period, since primary sources offer few details about the military organization of Argos. These few elements, however, are enough to create a general idea of how the Argive army was structured. For the Corinthian army, however, we have not a single fragment of information from the Classical period that could help in attempting a reconstruction

Thracian peltast with full national costume and weapons used by Thracian warriors. (*Photo and copyright by Athenea Prómakhos*)

Macedonian hoplite with bronze Attic helmet and 'muscle' cuirass. (*Photo and copyright by Athenea Prómakhos*)

of the military institutions of Corinth. Regarding the Argive army, we know that it was organized on five *lochoi*, having 1,000 hoplites each, and each *lochos* was commanded by a superior commander known as a *strategos*. Therefore, the standard Argive army on campaign comprised 5,000 hoplites. This structure on five *lochoi* was practically identical to that of the Spartan Army, since each *lochos* was in turn divided into twenty *pentekostyes* of fifty men each. Indeed, it was probably the Spartans who copied the Argives, since the latter's military structures were older than those of the Spartiates. We must remember that the famous *hoplon* was invented in Argos, and thus became known as the Argive shield, and that Argos was the dominant military power of the Peloponnese long before the ascendancy of Sparta. Like in Sparta, the five *lochoi* of hoplites were not recruited on a tribal basis. In 421 BC, after suffering several disastrous defeats in their clashes with the Spartans, the Argives decided to organize the largest corps of *Epilektoi* (professional soldiers) ever seen in Greece. With this new force, made up of 1,000 of the wealthiest and fittest young citizens, they hoped to deploy a corps comparable in quality and size to the Spartiates. The 1,000 picked hoplites were freed from all their public duties and were maintained by the public treasury so that they could devote their entire life to military training. Apparently, these elite soldiers were the first *Epilektoi* troops ever raised in mainland Greece.

Chapter 8

Panoply and Tactics of the Greek Armies

The Greek hoplites derived their name from the most important element of their personal equipment, the *hoplon* round shield. Also known as the Argive shield, its introduction during the last decades of the Greek Dark Ages marked the beginning of the so-called hoplite revolution. This kind of shield, differently from the previous ones that had been employed in mainland Greece during the Mycenean period, was quite convex and had a reinforced rim. In addition, it had an innovative grip that made its use particularly effective. This consisted of an arm band fitted to the centre of the shield on the back; the hoplite put his left forearm through the band and thus the shield was easily fastened. This simple but innovative system was completed by the presence of a strap, acting as a handgrip, near the rim. This was grasped with the left hand by the hoplite and made the danger of losing the shield unlikely, even during harsh close combat. These basic characteristics of the Argive shield, together with its dimensions – 80–100cm in diameter, covering a hoplite from the chin to the knee – made possible the introduction of hoplite tactics. Half of the *hoplon* always protruded beyond the left hand side of its user and thus could protect the right-hand side of the hoplite fighting next to him. If the hoplites were well trained, and a soldier had a good degree of coordination with the two comrades fighting on his sides, the phalanx worked perfectly as an impenetrable wall of shields.

Each shield was made of hardwood and was covered with bronze or ox-hide on the external surface. The rim and arm band were made of bronze, while all the other fittings attached to the back of it, including the hand grip, were made of rawhide or felt. The back of the shield was lined with leather. The standard weight of a *hoplon* was about 7kg. The external surface could be painted with an infinite variety of symbols and decorations: these could be individual designs, reflecting the personal taste of a single hoplite, or collective ones that included the specific symbols of a particular clan, military unit or city. Over time, as individualism became a secondary factor in Greek warfare, city emblems became the most popular shield devices, generally consisting of the city's initial, such as *alpha* for Athens and *lambda* for Sparta (the Spartans called themselves Lakedaimonians). Other cities preferred using religious or traditional symbols, like the famous Club of Herakles for Thebes, Herakles being considered as the founder of the city. Animals (both real and fantastic), geometric patterns and everyday objects were also popular subjects. Sometimes the shield motifs were made of bronze and were painted before being applied on the external surface of the *hoplon*. During the whole period considered here, until the great military reforms of the Macedonian kings, the *hoplon* remained the same and did not change any of its features. The only innovation introduced after the Persian Wars was the use of a leather curtain that was attached to the bottom of the shield in order to protect the hoplite's legs from enemy arrows. During the campaigns against the Persians, many Greek infantrymen were wounded in that only part of the body that was not protected by the shield or the helmet and armour. Leather curtains became quite popular and were employed on a large scale by hoplites operating in Asia, while later, when the practice of wearing greaves declined, they also started to be commonly used in Greece.

The *hoplon* was not the only kind of shield employed by the Greek hoplites during this period, as some soldiers also used the so-called Boeotian shield. This was similar to the *hoplon* shield and had an overall circular shape, but differed from it in having two large scooped indentations, one on each side. Its name derives from the fact that it was popular in Boeotia and Thebes. Apparently, this kind of shield derived from the Dipylon shield of the earlier Mycenaean period, which had the same distinct shape with scooped indentantions and more or less the same general dimensions. The indentations allowed the shield's user to thrust and stab with his spear or sword from a position closer to the shield's centre, rather than having to reach around or over the shield in order to strike. In addition, the indentations significantly reduced the overall weight of the shield.

Another fundamental element in the defensive equipment of a hoplite was his body armour. At the beginning of this period, the standard armour worn by Greek hoplites was that commonly known as bell cuirass, due to its shape, or Argive cuirass, because its oldest example has been discovered in Argos. This kind of armour derived from the previous models employed during the late Mycenaean period and was introduced on a large scale during the closing phase of the Greek Dark Ages. It consisted of a front and a back plate made of bronze, simply decorated in the form of the anatomy of the torso: this decoration was very basic and consisted of just a few lines. The two plates were assembled together thanks to two tubular projections that were fitted into corresponding slots and held in position with two pins, and also by two loops placed at the bottom of the left side (one on the front plate and one on the back plate). The plates were held in position on the shoulders with two iron spikes placed on the front plate which passed through corresponding holes on the back plate. In addition, under the left arm and at the left hip, the rolled-over edge was opened up to form a channel that held the front plate of the cuirass in position. Around the neck, arm holes and bottom edge of the cuirass there were embossed ridges created by rolling forward the bronze. The overall shape of the cuirass resembled that of a bell, being much larger in the bottom half. The Argive cuirass was usually worn together with several additional components, which made it quite heavy but very effective: a semi-circular plate known as a *mitra*, suspended from a waistbelt worn under the cuirass and protecting the abdomen; shoulder guards; arm guards (for the right arm only); thigh guards; greaves; ankle guards; and foot guards. All these additional protections were made of bronze and could be decorated with incisions in the same fashion as the cuirass. These elements, derived from the Mycenaean panoply employed centuries before in Greece, literally made the early hoplites look like 'men of bronze', particularly when added to by a helmet and shield made from the same material. As time progressed, due to the new need for mobility and speed in combat, these additional defensive elements fell into disuse, apart from the greaves.

During the period 550–500 BC, the bell cuirass declined in popularity and was rapidly substituted with the new muscle cuirass, the external surface of which was sculpted with great detail in order to perfectly reproduce the anatomy of the torso. The new model of cuirass could be quite short, reaching the waist, or long enough to cover the abdomen. The new muscle cuirass also consisted of two separate plates made of bronze, but these were joined together at the sides and at the shoulders with hinges, with one half of the hinge attached to the front plate and the other half to the back plate. Usually there were six hinges on each cuirass: two on each side and one for each shoulder. On either side of each hinge there was a ring that was used to pull the two plates of the cuirass together. Generally speaking, the muscle cuirass was worn on a very large scale during the Persian Wars, but by 450 BC it was no longer the most common model of body protection. The hoplites started to feel the need for an increased level of mobility that could not be achieved while wearing heavy bronze cuirasses, which were also quite difficult and expensive to produce. As a result, by the outbreak of the Peloponnesian War, linen had become the standard material for producing corselets. To substitute the uncomfortable *mitra*, by the time of the Persian Wars the Greeks had already started to employ linen or leather in order to produce the so-called *pteruges*: strips or lappets assembled together to form a sort of defensive skirt which could be worn under the bronze cuirass. Since they were extremely effective, especially against enemy arrows, the *pteruges* soon became popular and also started to be employed to protect the shoulders and upper arms, being worn under the muscle cuirass on the shoulders.

The linothorax, or linen cuirass, i.e. a cuirass entirely made of linen, was already used during the Persian Wars and had the great advantage of being particularly light and easy to wear. It consisted of multiple layers of linen pressed and glued together in order to form a corselet about 0.5cm thick. This corselet extended down to the hips, and its lower part, from below the waist, had slits to make it easy to bend forward. These slits formed a line of *pteruges*, which were part of the main cuirass and not a separate component. Under the main corselet another layer was worn, and this also had *pteruges* but was stuck on the inside of the cuirass in a way that made it cover the gaps opened in the *pteruges* of the outer layer. The whole corselet was produced as a single-piece object and was wrapped around the torso before being tied together on the left side. A specifically designed U-shaped plate, always made of linen, was worn on the shoulders; this was fixed to the back of the corselet and pulled forward to protect the frontal part of the shoulders. Very soon after the appearance of the linen cuirass, the Greeks created an updated version known as the composite cuirass, which basically was a standard linen cuirass reinforced by adding bronze scales on its external surface. These scales were usually assembled in a large band around the waist, but they could also be placed in other points of the corselet, such as the shoulders or the loins. Sometimes a linen corselet could be entirely covered with bronze scales, but these costly examples of composite cuirass were probably quite rare.

By the end of the Peloponnesian War, most of the Greek hoplites fought without armour but only with helmet and shield, a general trend which changed only with the ascendancy of Philip II, who equipped all his new phalangists with linen corselets. As a result of this military reform, the Greek cities also re-equipped their soldiers with linen cuirasses or composite versions. The use of muscle cuirasses was never fully abandoned, but during the time of Philip II these were generally used only by military commanders or chosen military corps (*Epilektoi*). The body protection of a hoplite was usually completed by a pair of bronze greaves, which also covered the knees and were usually worn together with sandals, but could also be used by soldiers who went to the field of battle barefoot. Greaves could be decorated in many different ways, for example reproducing the anatomy of the lower leg or with geometric incisions. They could be pulled open and clipped onto the leg, or strapped around the back.

The defensive equipment of the standard Greek hoplite was completed by his helmet, which was made of bronze but could have several different shapes. Unlike body armour, the use of which was temporarily abandoned during some decades of the period being considered, helmets continued to be worn by the Greek hoplites from the time of the Persian Wars up to the Macedonian conquest of Greece. Basically, eight different models of helmet were employed by the Greeks from 500–350 BC: the Corinthian helmet, Chalcidian helmet, Attic helmet, Illyrian helmet, Phrygian/ Thracian helmet, Boeotian helmet, Pilos helmet and Konos helmet. The Corinthian helmet was introduced during the last phase of the Greek Dark Ages and remained the most popular model of helmet during most of the early Classical period, until the outbreak of the Peloponnesian War. As is clear from its name, it was probably designed for the first time in Corinth, although it should be remembered that it was part of the so-called 'archaic panoply' discovered at Argos, which also comprised an Argive shield and bell cuirass. The Corinthian helmet included a frontal plate that covered the entire face, providing an excellent protection to the wearer, but over time the need for better visibility and reduced weight led to the progressive abandonment of this model of helmet, substituted by new ones open on the face. The Corinthian helmet only had three thin slits in the plate protecting the face: two for the eyes and a vertical one for the mouth and nose. On the back, a large curved projection protected the nape of the neck. When not fighting, a hoplite would wear his Corinthian helmet tipped upward for comfort: this way most of his face would have been freed by the frontal plate, which would have assumed an oblique position. This practice gave rise to a series of variants of the Corinthian helmet, which became popular in Italy but not in Greece. Generally speaking, an Italo-Corinthian helmet was a Corinthian helmet designed to be always worn in the 'comfort position', and thus not covering the bottom part of the wearer's face. As a result, the frontal plate of the Italo-Corinthian helmets did not have the thin slits for the eyes, mouth and nose. One of the main characteristics of the Corinthian helmet was the presence of an indentation in the bottom edge dividing the jawline from the neckline, yet this was gradually replaced by a simple dart. The greatest fault of the early Corinthian helmets was that they made hearing practically impossible: as a result, the surface of the helmet located over the ears started to be cut away.

Before adopting this solution, several experiments were made and these led to the creation of a new helmet which derived directly from the Corinthian one: the Chalcidian helmet. The latter was probably designed for the first time in Chalcis and thus was extremely popular among hoplites from the large island of Euboea. It was lighter and less bulky than a Corinthian helmet, since it left the face and ears of the wearer completely free, with no frontal plate, so hearing and vision were much better compared with the Corinthian helmet. The Chalcidian helmet consisted of a hemispherical dome under which were a pair of cheek pieces and a neck guard, while on the front there was a very small nasal bar. The cheek pieces could be fixed or hinged to the helmet. Adornments and protuberances of various kinds could be attached to the top of the helmet's dome. Various experiments were made to improve the Chalcidian helmet, which led to the introduction of the Attic helmet: this, as is clear from its name, was widely used in the area of Attica and thus in Athens. It was one of the latest models of helmet to be developed during the Classical period and thus was greatly used during the subsequent Hellenistic period initiated by Alexander the Great. In general terms, the Attic helmet was quite similar to the Chalcidian one, but without the latter's nose guard. Cheek pieces were hinged and not fixed, as in the later examples of Chalcidian helmet. The Attic helmet became extremely popular in Italy and, over time, started to be decorated in a variety of ways: these included incisions, adornments and protuberances of various kinds that were sculpted or applied on its external surface.

The Corinthian, Chalcidian and Attic helmets were all linked together and were part of a common evolutionary process that started during the Greek Dark Ages. At the same time, in addition to the Corinthian one, another kind of helmet was also developed: the Illyrian helmet. This evolved from the so-called *Kegelhelm* (a cone- or skittle-shaped helmet) produced during the Archaic period in Central Europe and brought into the southern Balkans by the Illyrians. Examples of the Illyrian helmet discovered in Argos have been dated to the same period which saw the introduction of the Argive panoply (Corinthian helmet, bell cuirass and Argive shield). The Illyrian helmet was produced in four different variants during the period 700–500 BC and was no longer used by the early fifth century BC. All four variants were characterized by the presence of two ridges running across the dome from the back of the head to the front, used to support the helmet's crest. In addition, all of them left the face completely free since they had no frontal plate. The first variant, produced until 650 BC, left the neck unprotected and hampered hearing; the second one, produced until 600 BC, introduced neck protection but continued to hamper hearing; the third variant, produced until 550 BC, offered neck protection and improved hearing; and the last one, produced until 500 BC, had neck protection and left the ears completely free.

The Phrygian/Thracian, Boeotian and Pilos helmets all derived from soft caps that were worn by the Greeks during their everyday life. The first model, the Phrygian/Thracian helmet, started to be produced after the Greeks came in close contact with the warriors inhabiting Thrace and Phrygia, the latter being a region of Anatolia that was populated by a warlike community of Thracian stock that had migrated from Thrace to Asia Minor during the Archaic period of Greek history. Both the Thracians and Phrygians wore the same distinct soft cap, having a high and forward-inclined apex. The model of helmet deriving from this cap had the same apex and was characterized by the presence of a peak at the front, which shaded the wearer's eyes and offered some additional protection. Sometimes, instead of the peak, a Phrigyan/Thracian helmet could have a small nasal bar similar to the one on the Chalcidian helmets. A couple of large cheek pieces were attached to the main body of the helmet, and frequently these were large enough to form a facial mask, leaving only three small gaps for the eyes, nose and mouth. When the cheek pieces were large and linked together to form this mask, the overall appearance of the helmet was not so different from that of the Corinthian one. All the helmets described until now were usually decorated with crests of horse hair, attached with props, pins, hooks or rings.

The Boeotian helmet, as indicated by its name, was first developed in the region of Boeotia and thus was extremely popular in Thebes. Despite being largely used by Boeotian hoplites, it became extremely common as a cavalry helmet and was also adopted by the Athenian cavalry. In many aspects it was absolutely perfect for cavalry use: it was completely open on the face, allowed good peripheral vision and permitted unimpaired hearing. The Boeotian helmet consisted of a domed skull surrounded by a wide and flaring down-sloping brim. The latter came down at the rear to protect the back of the neck, but also projected forward over the forehead to work as a sort of visor. On the sides the brim had a complex shape, comprising downward-pointing folds that protected the lateral areas of the face. Basically, the Boeotian helmet was a bronze version of the usual *Petasos* sun hat, which was widely employed by the Thessalian cavalry. In particular, it had the same shape as the Boeotian version of the *Petasos*, which was employed by the Boeotian cavalry and was characterized by the presence of the downward-pointing folds on the sides. This kind of helmet was usually decorated with a falling horsehair plume instead of a crest. The Pilos helmet was a bronze version of the famous cap of the same name, which was worn by most of the Greek peasants during their everyday life. The Pilos was a brimless skullcap made of felt, having a simple conical shape. When at war, hoplites generally wore their Pilos cap under the helmet for increased comfort, as a result of which a new model of helmet with exactly the same shape as the cap started to be developed. This was very comfortable to wear and easy to produce, to the point that by the end of the Peloponnesian War it had become the most common model of helmet produced in Greece and been adopted by the Spartan army as its standard helmet. The Pilos helmet was quite tall and thus offered good protection for an infantryman against cavalry. In addition, it was completely open and thus gave full vision to its wearer, only having a small visor around the opening. The Konos helmet was the very last model of helmet developed during the Classical period and saw large use during the following Hellenistic period. Basically, it was a variation of the Pilos helmet, but with two main peculiarities: instead of the visor, it had a thin brim protruding from the base and closely fitting around the wearer's head, and frequently it also had bronze ear guards that hung to the jawbone. In practice, it was a Pilos helmet with the characteristic brim of a Boeotian one and additional ear guards.

The hoplite's main weapon was his spear, the *dory*, which was 2–3 metres long, with both its head and butt made of iron. The blade of the head was leaf-shaped, while the spike placed at the butt end was very thin and could be used to strike as well as to fix the spear into the ground. Each hoplite used his sword only when his spear was broken in combat, so it could be consider as a secondary weapon. The Greek soldiers of the Classical period used two different models of sword, both short and made of iron: the *Kopis* and the *Xiphos*. The *Kopis* was a heavy cutting sword with a forward-curving blade that was single-edged. One-handed, it had a blade length of 48–65cm, which pitched forward towards the point and was concave on the part located nearest to the hilt. The peculiar re-curved shape of the *Kopis* made it capable of delivering a blow with the same power as an axe. A peculiar version of the *Kopis*, known as the *Machaira*, also existed: this had all the same features as the former, but its blade was not re-curved. The *Kopis* was particularly appreciated as a cavalry weapon, due to the peculiar shape of its blade, while the *Machaira* was primarily an infantry sword. The universal sword of the hoplites, however, was without doubt the *Xiphos*, a one-handed and double-edged short sword with a straight blade that measured between 45cm and 60cm. It usually had a midrib and was diamond or lenticular in cross-section. The *Xiphos* had quite a long point and thus was an excellent thrusting weapon specifically designed for close combat.

Bibliography

Primary sources

Arrian, *Tactics*

Asklepiodotos, *Tactics*

Diodorus Siculus, *History*

Herodotus, *The Histories*

Livy, *History of Rome from its foundation*

Pausanias, *Guide to Greece*

Plutarch, *Lives*

Polybius, *The Histories*

Strabo, *Geography*

Thucydides, *History of the Peloponnesian War*

Xenophon, *Anabasis*

Xenophon, *Hellenica*

Xenophon, *Kyropaidia*

Xenophon, *On horsemanship*

Xenophon, *The cavalry commander*

Secondary sources

Campbell, D., *Spartan Warrior 735–331 BC* (Osprey Publishing, 2012)

Cassin-Scott, J., *The Greek and Persian Wars 500–323 BC* (Osprey Publishing, 1977)

Cernenko, E.V., *The Scythians 700–300 BC* (Osprey Publishing, 1983)

Connolly, P., *The Greek Armies* (Macdonald Educational, 1977)

Connolly, P., *Greece and Rome at War* (Prentice-Hall, 1981)

Everson, T., *Warfare in Ancient Greece: Arms and Armour from the Heroes of Homer to Alexander the Great* (The History Press, 2005)

Gorelik, K., *Warriors of Eurasia* (Montvert Publishing, 1995)

Head, D., *Armies of the Macedonian and Punic Wars* (Wargames Research Group, 1982)

Kagan, D. and Viggiano, G.F., *Men of Bronze: Hoplite Warfare in Ancient Greece* (Princeton University Press, 2013)

Lazenby, J.F., *The Spartan Army* (Stackpole Books, 2012)

Middleton, H., *Ancient Greek War and Weapons* (Heinemann/Raintree, 2002)

Nelson, R., *Armies of the Greek and Persian Wars* (Wargames Research Group, 1978)

Quesada Sanz, F., *Armas de Grecia y Roma* (La Esfera, 2014)

Sage, M., *Warfare in Ancient Greece: a Sourcebook* (Psychology Press, 1996)

Sekunda, N., *The Ancient Greeks* (Osprey Publishing, 1986)

Sekunda, N., *The Spartan Army* (Osprey Publishing, 1998)

Sekunda, N., *Greek Hoplite 480–323 BC* (Osprey Publishing, 2000)

Tomlinson, R., *Argos and the Argolid* (Routledge, 1972)

Warry, J., *Warfare in the Classical World* (Salamander Books, 1997)

Webber, C., *The Thracians 700 BC–AD 46* (Osprey Publishing, 2001)

The Re-enactors who Contributed to this Book

Athenea Prómakhos

Athenea Prómakhos was created in Saragossa, Spain, during 2004, having as its main objective that of recreating and divulging the history and daily life of the ancient Greek warriors. The group was officially registered as a non-profit cultural association in April 2006. In Greek mythology, Athenea (Athena) was the goddess of wisdom, skill and the arts; for this reason, together with Apollo, she was the religious entity who best represented the national spirit of the ancient Greeks. In addition, Athenea was also a warrior-goddess, having the term *Prómakhos* (i.e., warrior) among her most important attributes. Differently from the blind violence and thirst for blood that characterized the fighting style of her brother Mars, Athenea's military performances were guided by great intelligence and she usually preferred peaceful solutions to war, whenever possible. The association derives its name exactly from this peculiar faculty of Athenea (i.e., Athenea the warrior). Athenea Prómakhos has grown considerably and now comprises many members living in every corner of Spain. The association has not only expanded from a numerical point of view, but also from a qualitative one. It has greatly augmented the topics covered by its activities: after years of research and practical experience, the group is by now able to cover all general aspects of the ancient Greeks' daily life. This means that the activities performed by the association are not focused only on military aspects, but also on those that characterized the civil life of the Greek communities. In addition, the members of Athenea Prómakhos can now also reconstruct the daily life of the foreign communities that came into contact with the Greeks, either as allies or enemies. These had a great influence over the development of Greek civilization, and their main features had a deep impact on the evolution of Greek culture across the centuries. All the activities of Athenea Prómakhos are based on accurate research and analysis of all the most important primary sources dating back to the Classical period, be they literary or archaeological. Its researches are obviously supplemented by the methodical consultation of all the scientific publications dedicated to the history and archaeology of Ancient Greece, and by frequent visits to some of the world's most important museums dedicated to Greek civilization. Members of the association have thus been able to develop a direct and evidence-based knowledge of the objects that they recreate. The latter is constantly enriched by their participation in important historical and archaeological conferences, as well as by the frequent contacts that the association has with important historians and archaeologists of the Greek world. The main objective of Athenea Prómakhos is that of using a true philological approach in all its re-enacting activities, in order to reproduce the materials and objects in the best possible way and to perform activities of top quality. All this is made without renouncing the original spirit of historical re-enacting, which comprises important social aspects. Thanks to its researches and activities, which have experienced great success over the years, its members have been able to participate in important and prestigious events in various European countries, among which have been Tarraco Viva, Les Grands Jeux Romaines of Nîmes, re-enacting events at Aquileia and the 2,500th anniversary of the Battle of Marathon in Greece. Athenea Prómakhos has also performed at important museums and archaeological sites, such as El Efebo in Agde, Saint-Romain-en-Gal, Loupian, Olbia and Ampurias. The group is always open to any kind of collaboration aimed at the divulging of historical and archaeological knowledge related to Greek civilization.

Contacts:
apromakhos@gmail.com
www.atheneapromakhos.org
https://www.facebook.com/groups/799282110120899/

Index